Gallery Books
General Editor: Peter Fallon

SELECTED POEMS OF
JAMES CLARENCE MANGAN

Selected Poems
of
James Clarence Mangan

Edited by Michael Smith
with a foreword by
Anthony Cronin

Gallery Books

A version of Anthony Cronin's essay appeared
in *Hibernia,* May 1972.

The Gallery Press
Peter Fallon,
19, Oakdown Road,
Dublin 14. Ireland.

Contents

Editor's Note

James Clarence Mangan was the first modern Irish poet. Catholic, poor, of the people, republican, nationalist, dreamer, talented and weak-willed, European and good Dubliner, weaver of exotic tapestries at the cliff's edge, the failed man and the fallen angel, soul-brother of Poe, B.V.,[1] Baudelaire and Verlaine.

Mangan is more than his poems, as the saint is more than his printed prayers. It was Mangan's bad luck to have been born at a time when the English language, after the debilitating, fashionable excesses of Byron, was in a state of almost irredeemable decadence. He should, of course, have been born into French or Spanish or Italian or Persian. Fit for a palace, he had to survive in a hovel.

For the modern Irish poet, the figure of Mangan has a very special significance. Mangan, filled with the importance of poetry through the fame of Shelley and Byron, deceived by provincial Dublin's 18th century grandeur, tried to live as a poet. The result was then, as it would be now, the poet reduced by a materialist, cynical society to a broken man, laughing-stock, alcoholic, drug addict, weirdo, degenerate, hopeless case, victim.

It was Mangan's triumph that with a shoddy language, a heartlessly indifferent public, beset by poverty without and weakness within, he somehow managed to write a handful of good poems. The present editor is presumptuous enough to think that this book contains that handful . . . and more besides. Anthony Cronin remarks in his characteristically perceptive foreword, 'Mangan seems most of the time not to be making any attempt to bring the whole man in.' Agreeing with this, the editor has decided, circumspectly, he hopes, to include a number of poems which, though not up to closely critical reading, help to substantiate the figure behind such poems as *The Nameless One.*'

The editor being no scholar, this is not a scholarly edition of Mangan's poems. What is here presented to the public — for the first time in many decades — is what the editor thinks is of permanent literary value in the poems of Mangan, drawing, in the main, on O'Donoghue's *Poems of James Clarence Mangan.*

Michael Smith

---

1. James Thompson (1834-82), author of 'The City of Dreadful Night.'

9

Foreword

Some twenty years or so after James Clarence Mangan's death, the young Arthur Rimbaud, who, of course, had never heard of him, invented the notion of the poet as *maudit*, "accursed." Suffering was an essential part of his role, and it was actually necessary for the poet to deliberately become *"le grand malade, le grand criminal, le grand maudit."* Part of the concept, subsequently developed by Verlaine, and adopted, consciously or otherwise, by many poets, (the otherwise often leading to strange results) was that of the poet as scapegoat, who, by sin and circumstance, getting himself into trouble and generally bashed around, atoned in some way for the sins and hypocrises of society. It was primarily related to the obvious hypocrises of bourgeois society, which was felt by both parties to the contract to be deeply in need of such an animal as a scapegoat. One says both parties for, of course, society gleefully, if inchoately, adopted the idea.

Thus, every country has its sacrificial poets. France has Baudelaire, Verlaine, and Rimbaud himself. America got off to a good start with Edgar Allen Poe and kept it up with Hart Crane and others. If the major English poets of the nineteenth century were far too disposed towards comfort to accept the role of scapegoat, in the nineties a whole generation, including Ernest Dowson, Lionel Johnson and Oscar Wilde cheerfully rushed in to supply a long-felt want. (Yeats's references to Dowson and Johnson suggest some guilt on his part about holding back.) The public rejoicings on both sides of the Atlantic which greeted the final self-destruction of even such a poet as Dylan Thomas demonstrated the strength of the feeling of need. Aspects of Dylan's own psychology amply demonstrated that he wanted the role.

And Ireland? Well, Ireland has James Clarence Mangan; and, though the poet himself frequently waved aside the proferred purple, Patrick Kavanagh. The late Brendan Behan somewhat incongruously tried to get in on this act too. The role as such is not in fact a dishonourable one, and the idea has much to commend it. It was invented by a considerable fellow and poets understand it. Of course, suffering is not enough. As has often been made clear, anybody who has money enough to go out and collect a hangover, or get himself muddled up sexually, can do the suffering. Still, there is some sort of necessity in the thing, a religious necessity felt by the poets, whatever about society's motives. They are, I suppose one could demonstrate, a perfect perversion of certain religious feelings. And the idea of poet as *maudit* is also a modern one, related to the industrial revolution, materialism, progress and,

11

of course, to the loss by the poet of his true, or at least his old, role. To make the claim for Mangan that he partially at least knew what it was all about, is to suggest that he was a modern poet.

He has, of course, been ill served by the anthologists, all of them content to take in each other's washing. The representation of Mangan in Irish anthologies would seem extraordinarily repetitive, except that everything in Irish anthologies seems so. "My Dark Rosaleen," whatever else one thinks of it, is not a modern poem: that is to say it does not relate to any experience realised by anybody walking the streets today. A product of two romanticisms, the literary one and the nationalist one, it is a fair old performance of a kind, but anybody who thinks of Ireland as a maiden, "a saint of saints," making "sweet and sad complaints," whose "holy delicate white hands" will "girdle him with steel" wants to have the general mechanism of his sensibility examined.

Nor is Mangan well served by his own prolixity and general indeterminacy of purpose and style. Yeats pointed out quite properly that the establishment of a style, even though it might vary at periods of the poet's life, was half the battle. He also remarked rather sadly on the fact that it is possible to bring to birth in verse only a very small amount of one's personality. Mangan seems most of the time not to be making any attempt to bring the whole man in. Part of the trouble here is that he was in fact early in the game with a specifically modern notion: that of operating behind masks and personae. All those fake or partial translations, the pretence that poems were from the Ottoman, the Turkish, the Persian, the Arabic, the German, the Irish even (of which he knew very little) may be seen as a rudimentary attempt to use the mask in what is really quite a modern way: the way it is used in "Homage to Sextus Propertius," etc.

At least once he used it superbly. "Twenty Golden Years Ago," attributed to the non-existent Selber, in other words the self, is an astonishingly modern poem and it establishes Mangan at once as a contemporary whose pain and remorse we can understand. The circumstances are not his but they are real. The imagery is urban; there are no stock properties; no grots, vales or bowers, and nothing, from the coffee in the cup onwards, is too mundane to be worthy of inclusion. The tone is kept low deliberately; the self-mockery is unindulgent and bitterly ironic, in fact we might almost be in the country of Laforgue, Corbiere and the Eliot of "Prufrock"; there is no romantic agony, but there is a real agony all the same; and it jumps out of the pages that surround it in poor Mangan's works.

12

He wrote really a great many more good poems than the anthologists seem to be aware of, but only once did he equal this. "The Nameless One" seems to me to be the only occasion on which he drops the masks entirely, including the romantic masks, Byronic and otherwise, that the poor fellow, in his general weakness of poetic will, perhaps did not know he was adopting. It might be thought to begin badly with the rhetorical apostrophe to the song to "roll forth . . . Like a rushing river," etcetera, but the rhythm, even if it is only a slight variation on stock rhythms, is altogether Mangan's own. Here is the personal rhythm that is the sure mark of the genuine article. The tone is rhetorical, but it is extraordinary how mundane circumstance prevails at the same time. He admits to the drink, "gulf and grave of Maginn and Burns"; he tells us his age and condition, "old and hoary at thirty-nine"; and he tells us what his life is like: "want and sickness and houseless nights." There is nothing rarer in poetry than a successful cry from the whole encircumstanced heart. This is one.

These two poems seem to me to be not only the first two modern poems written in Ireland in the English language, but among the first in that language anywhere. For once Mangan gets his real agony on paper and it is a modern agony. It is extraordinary that they should have been written in the eighteen forties. Between the drink and the opium and a hideous romantic love of despair, poor Mangan brought a lot on himself, and he rarely succeeded in bringing that self to poetic birth. The suffering in "The Nameless One" has a terrible intensity. He was, if the concept has any truth in it, *maudit* all right.

Anthony Cronin

13

The Poems

Dark Rosaleen[1]

(From the Irish of Costello)

O My Dark Rosaleen,
  Do not sigh, do not weep!
The priests are on the ocean green,
  They march along the Deep.
There's wine . . . from the royal Pope
  Upon the ocean green;
And Spanish ale shall give you hope,
  My Dark Rosaleen!
  My own Rosaleen!
Shall glad your heart, shall give you hope,
Shall give you health, and help, and hope,
  My Dark Rosaleen.

1. Mangan says this poem was entitled in the original Roisin Dubh, and was written in the reign of Elizabeth by one of the poets of Red Hugh O'Donnell, and is supposed to be addressed to Ireland by that famous chieftain.

Over hills and through dales
  Have I roamed for your sake;
All yesterday I sailed with sails
  On river and on lake.
The Erne . . . at its highest flood
  I dashed across unseen,
For there was lightning in my blood,
  My Dark Rosaleen!
  My own Rosaleen!
Oh! there was lightning in my blood,
Red lightning lightened through my blood,
  My Dark Rosaleen!

All day long in unrest
  To and fro do I move,
The very soul within my breast
  Is wasted for you, love!
The heart . . . in my bosom faints
  To think of you, my Queen,
My life of life, my saint of saints,
  My Dark Rosaleen!
  My own Rosaleen!
To hear your sweet and sad complaints,
My life, my love, my saint of saints,
  My Dark Rosaleen!

Woe and pain, pain and woe,
  Are my lot night and noon,
To see your bright face clouded so,
  Like to the mournful moon.
But yet . . . will I rear your throne
  Again in golden sheen;
'Tis you shall reign, shall reign alone,
  My Dark Rosaleen!
  My own Rosaleen!
'Tis you shall have the golden throne,
'Tis you shall reign, and reign alone,
  My Dark Rosaleen!

Over dews, over sands
   Will I fly for your weal;
Your holy delicate white hands
   Shall girdle me with steel.
At home ... in your emerald bowers,
   From morning's dawn till e'en,
You'll pray for me, my flower of flowers,
   My Dark Rosaleen!
   My fond Rosaleen!
You'll think of me through Daylight's hours,
My virgin flower, my flower of flowers,
   My Dark Rosaleen!

I could scale the blue air,
   I could plough the high hills,
Oh, I could kneel all night in prayer,
   To heal your many ills!
And one ... beamy smile from you
   Would float like light between
My toils and me, my own, my true,
   My Dark Rosaleen!
   My fond Rosaleen!
Would give me life and soul anew,
A second life, a soul anew,
   My Dark Rosaleen!

O! the Erne shall run red
   With redundance of blood,
The earth shall rock beneath our tread,
   And flames wrap hill and wood,
And gun-peal, and slogan cry,
   Wake many a glen serene,
Ere you shall fade, ere you shall die,
   My Dark Rosaleen!
   My own Rosaleen!
The Judgment Hour must first be nigh,
Ere you can fade, ere you can die,
   My Dark Rosaleen!

O'Hussey's Ode to the Maguire[1]

(*From the Irish of O'Hussey*)

Where is my Chief, my Master, this bleak night, *mavrone*!
O, cold, cold, miserably cold is this bleak night for Hugh,
It's showery, arrowy, speary sleet pierceth one through and through,
Pierceth one to the very bone!

Rolls real thunder? Or was that red, livid light
Only a meteor? I scarce know; but through the midnight dim
The pitiless ice-wind streams. Except the hate that persecutes *him*
Nothing hath crueller venomy might.

An awful, a tremendous night is this, meseems!
The flood-gates of the rivers of heaven, I think, have been burst
    wide—
Down from the overcharged clouds, like unto headlong ocean's tide,
Descends grey rain in roaring streams.

Though he were even a wolf ranging the round green woods,
Though he were even a pleasant salmon in the unchainable sea,
Though he were a wild mountain eagle, he could scarce bear, he,
This sharp, sore sleet, these howling floods.

O, mournful is my soul this night for Hugh Maguire!
Darkly, as in a dream, he strays! Before him and behind
Triumphs the tyrannous anger of the wounding wind,
The wounding wind, that burns as fire!

It is my bitter grief — it cuts me to the heart —
That in the country of Clan Darry this should be his fate!
O, woe is me, where is he? Wandering, houseless, desolate,
Alone, without or guide or chart!

---

1. O'Hussey was the last hereditary bard of the Maguire sect.

Medreams I see just now his face, the strawberry bright,
Uplifted to the blackened heavens, while the tempestuous winds
Blow fiercely over and round him, and the smiting sleet-shower
    blinds
The hero of Galang to-night!

Large, large affliction unto me and mine it is,
That one of his majestic bearing, his fair, stately form,
Should thus be tortured and o'erborne — that this unsparing storm
Should wreak its wrath on head like his!

That his great hand, so oft the avenger of the oppressed,
Should this chill, churlish night, perchance, be paralysed by frost—
While through some icicle-hung thicket—as one lorn and lost—
He walks and wanders without rest.

The tempest-driven torrent deluges the mead,
It overflows the low banks of the rivulets and ponds—
The lawns and pasture-grounds lie locked in icy bonds
So that the cattle cannot feed.

The pale bright margins of the streams are seen by none.
Rushes and sweeps along the untamable flood on every side—
It penetrates and fills the cottagers' dwellings far and wide—
Water and land are blent in one.

Through some dark woods, 'mid bones of monsters, Hugh now
    strays,
As he confronts the storm with anguished heart, but manly brow—
O! what a sword-wound to that tender heart of his were now
A backward glance at peaceful days.

But other thoughts are his—thoughts that can still inspire
With joy and an onward-bounding hope the bosom of Mac-Nee—
Thoughts of his warriors charging like bright billows of the sea,
Borne on the wind's wings, flashing fire!

And though frost glaze to-night the clear dew of his eyes,
And white ice-gauntlets glove his noble fine fair fingers o'er,
A warm dress is to him that lightning-garb he ever wore,
The lightning of the soul, not skies.

Avran[1]

Hugh marched forth to the fight—I grieved to see him so depart;
And lo! to-night he wanders frozen, rain-drenched, sad, betrayed—
But the memory of the lime-white mansions his right hand hath laid
In ashes warms the hero's heart!

The Woman of Three Cows

(*From the Irish*)

O woman of Three Cows, *agra*! don't let your tongue thus rattle!
O, don't be saucy, don't be stiff, because you may have cattle.
I have seen—and, here's my hand to you, I only say what's true—
A many a one with twice your stock not half so proud as you.

Good luck to you, don't scorn the poor, and don't be their despiser,
For worldly wealth soon melts away, and cheats the very
    miser,
And Death soon strips the proudest wreath from haughty
    human brows;
Then don't be stiff, and don't be proud, good Woman of Three
    Cows.

---

1. A concluding stanza, generally intended as a recapitulation of the entire poem.

20

See where Momonia's heroes lie, proud Owen More's descendants,
'Tis they that won the glorious name, and had the grand attendants!
If *they* were forced to bow to Fate, as every mortal bows,
Can *you* be proud, can *you* be stiff, my Woman of Three Cows!

The brave sons of the Lord of Clare, they left the land to mourning;
Mavrone! for they were banished, with no hope of their returning—
Who knows in what abodes of want those youths were driven to
     house?
Yet *you* can give yourself these airs, O Woman of Three Cows!

O, think of Donnell of the Ships, the Chief whom nothing daunted—
See how he fell in distant Spain, unchronicled, unchanted!
He sleeps, the great O'Sullivan, where thunder cannot rouse—
Then ask yourself, should *you* be proud, good Woman of Three
     Cows!

O'Ruark, Maguire, those souls of fire, whose names are shrined
     in story—
Think how their high achievements once made Erin's highest
     glory—
Yet now their bones lie mouldering under weeds and cypress
     boughs,
And so, for all your pride, will yours, O Woman of Three Cows!

The O'Carrolls, also, famed when Fame was only for the boldest,
Rest in forgotten sepulchres with Erin's best and oldest;
Yet who so great as they of yore in battle or carouse?
Just think of that, and hide your head, good Woman of Three
     Cows!

Your neighbour's poor, and you, it seems, are big with vain ideas,
Because, *inagh*![1] you've got three cows—one more, I see, than
     she has.
That tongue of yours wags more at times than Charity allows,
But if you're strong, be merciful, great Woman of Three Cows!

1. Forsooth.

21

Now, there you go! You still, of course, keep up your scornful
    bearing,
And I'm too poor to hinder you; but, by the cloak I'm wearing,
If I had but *four* cows myself, even though you were my spouse,
I'd thwack you well to cure your pride, my Woman of Three Cows!

Lament over the Ruins of the Abbey of Teach Molaga[1]

(From the Irish)

I wandered forth at night alone
Along the dreary, shingly, billow-beaten shore;
Sadness that night was in my bosom's core,
    My soul and strength lay prone.

The thin wan moon, half overveiled
By clouds, shed her funereal beams upon the scene;
While in low tones, with many a pause between,
    The mournful night-wind wailed.

Musing of Life, and Death, and Fate,
I slowly paced along, heedless of aught around,
Till on the hill, now, alas! ruin-crowned,
    Lo! the old Abbey-gate!

Dim in the pallid moonlight stood,
Crumbling to slow decay, the remnant of that pile
Within which dwelt so many saints erewhile
    In loving brotherhood!

1.   Timoleague, Co. Cork.

The memory of the men who slept
Under those desolate walls—the solitude—the hour—
Mine own lorn mood of mind—all joined to o'erpower
    My spirit—and I wept!

In yonder Goshen once—I thought—
Reigned Piety and Peace: Virtue and Truth were there;
With Charity and the blessed spirit of Prayer
    Was each fleet moment fraught!

There, unity of Work and Will
Blend hundreds into one : no jealousies or jars
Troubled their placid lives : their fortunate stars
    Had triumphed o'er all Ill!

There, kneeled each morn and even
The Bell for Matin—Vesper : Mass was said or sung—
From the bright silver censer as it swung
    Rose balsamy clouds to Heaven.

Through the round cloistered corridors
A many a midnight hour, bareheaded and unshod,
Walked the Grey Friars, beseeching from their God
    Peace for these western shores.

The weary pilgrim bowed by Age
Oft found asylum there—found welcome, and found wine.
Oft rested in its halls the Paladine,
    The Poet and the Sage!

Alas! alas! how dark the change!
Now round its mouldering walls, over its pillars low,
The grass grows rank, the yellow gowans blow,
    Looking so sad and strange!

Unsightly stones choke up its wells;
The owl hoots all night long under the altar-stairs;
The fox and badger make their darksome lairs
    In its deserted cells!

Tempest and Time—the drifting sands—
The lightning and the rains—the seas that sweep around
These hills in winter-nights, have awfully crowned
　　The work of impious hands!

　　The sheltering, smooth-stoned massive wall—
The noble figured roof—the glossy marble piers—
The monumental shapes of elder years—
　　Where are they? Vanished all!

　　Rite, incense, chant, prayer, mass, have ceased—
All, all have ceased! Only the whitening bones half sunk
In the earth now tell that ever here dwelt monk,
　　Friar, acolyte, or priest.

　　Oh! woe, that Wrong should triumph thus!
Woe that the olden right, the rule and the renown
Of the Pure-souled and Meek should thus go down
　　Before the Tyrannous!

　　Where wert thou, Justice, in that hour?
Where was thy smiting sword? What had those good men
　　done,
That thou shouldst tamely see them trampled on
　　By brutal England's Power?

　　Alas! I rave! . . . If Change is here,
Is it not o'er the land? Is it not too in me?
Yes! I am changed even more than what I see.
　　Now is my last goal near!

　　My worn limbs fail—my blood moves cold—
Dimness is on mine eyes—I have seen my children die;
They lie where I too in brief space shall lie—
　　Under the grassy mould!

　　I turned away, as toward my grave,
And, all my dark way homeward by the Atlantic's verge,
Resounded in mine ears like to a dirge
　　The roaring of the wave.

The Geraldine's Daughter

(*From the Irish of Egan O'Rahilly*)

A beauty all stainless, a pearl of a maiden,
    Has plunged me in trouble, and wounded my heart;
With sorrow and gloom is my soul overladen,
    An anguish is there that will never depart.
I would voyage to Egypt across the deep water,
    Nor care about bidding dear Eire farewell,
So I only might gaze on the Geraldine's daughter,
    And sit by her side in some green, pleasant dell !

Her curling locks wave round her figure of lightness,
    All dazzling and long, like the purest of gold;
Her blue eyes resemble twin stars in their brightness,
    And her brow is like marble or wax to behold.
The radiance of heaven illumines her features
    Where the snows and the rose have erected their throne;
It would seem that the sun had forgotten all creatures,
    To shine on the Geraldine's daughter alone.

Her bosom is swan-white, her waist smooth and slender;
    Her speech is like music, so sweet and so fair;
The feelings that glow in her noble heart lend her
    A mien and a majesty lovely to see.
Her lips, red as berries, but riper than any,
    Would kiss away even a sorrow like mine !
No wonder such heroes and noblemen many
    Should cross the blue ocean to kneel at her shrine.

She is sprung from the Geraldine race, the great Grecians,
    Niece of Mileadh's sons of the Valorous Bands,
Those heroes, the seed of the olden Phoenicians,
    Though now trodden down, without fame, without lands;
Of her ancestors flourished the Barrys and Powers,
    To the Lords of Bunratty she, too, is allied,
And not a proud noble near Cashel's high towers
    But is kin to this maiden, the Geraldine's pride.

Of Saxon or Gael there is none to excel in
    Her wisdom, her features, her figure, this fair;
In all she surpasses the far-famed Helen,
    Whose beauty drove thousands to death and despair.
Whoe'er could but gaze on her aspect so noble
    Would feel from thenceforward all anguish depart;
Yet for me 'tis, alas ! my worst woe and my trouble
    That her image must always abide in my heart !

A Vision of Connaught in the Thirteenth Century

I walked entranced
    Through a land of Morn;
The sun, with wondrous excess of light,
    Shone down and glanced
    Over seas of corn
And lustrous gardens aleft and right.
    Even in the clime
    Of resplendent Spain,
Beams no such sun upon such a land;
    But it was the time,
    'Twas in the reign,
Of Cáhal Mór of the Wine-red Hand.

Anon stood nigh
    By my side a man
Of princely aspect and port sublime.
    Him queried I —
    "O, my Lord and Khan,[1]
What clime is this, and what golden time ?"
    When he — "The clime
    Is a clime to praise,
The clime is Erin's, the green and bland;
    And it is the time,
    These be the days,
Of Cáhal Mór of the Wine-red Hand!"

1.   *Ceann,* the Gaelic title for a chief.

Then saw I thrones,
  And circling fires,
And a Dome rose near me, as by a spell,
  Whence flowed the tones
    Of silver lyres,
And many voices in wreathèd swell;
  And their thrilling chime
    Fell on mine ears
As the heavenly hymn of an angel-band —
  "It is now the time,
    These be the years,
Of Cáhal Mór of the Wine-red Hand!"

I sought the hall,
  And, behold ! — a change
From light to darkness, from joy to woe !
  King, nobles, all,
    Looked aghast and strange;
The minstrel-group sate in dumbest show!
  Had some great crime
    Wrought this dread amaze,
This terror ? None seemed to understand
  'Twas then the time,
    We were in the days,
Of Cáhal Mór of the Wine-red Hand.

I again walked forth;
  But lo ! the sky
Showed fleckt with blood, and an alien sun
  Glared from the north,
    And there stood on high,
Amid his shorn beams, a skeleton !
  It was by the stream
    Of the castled Maine,
One Autumn eve, in the Teuton's land,
  That I dreamed this dream
    Of the time and reign
Of Cáhal Mór of the Wine-red Hand!

The Nameless One

Ballad

Roll forth, my song, like the rushing river,
  That sweeps along to the mighty sea;
God will inspire me while I deliver
  My soul of thee !

Tell thou the world, when my bones lie whitening
  Amid the last homes of youth and eld,
That there was once one whose veins ran lightning
  No eye beheld.

Tell how his boyhood was one drear night-hour,
  How shone for *him,* through his griefs and gloom,
No star of all heaven sends to light our
  Path to the tomb.

Roll on, my song, and to after ages
  Tell how, disdaining all earth can give,
He would have taught men, from wisdom's pages,
  The way to live.

And tell how trampled, derided, hated,
  And worn by weakness, disease, and wrong,
He fled for shelter to God, who mated
  His soul with song —

With song which alway, sublime or vapid,
  Flowed like a rill in the morning beam,
Perchance not deep, but intense and rapid —
  A mountain stream.

Tell how this Nameless, condemned for years long
  To herd with demons from hell beneath,
Saw things that made him, with groans and tears, long
  For even death.

Go on to tell how, with genius wasted,
  Betrayed in friendship, befooled in love,
With spirit shipwrecked, and young hopes blasted,
  He still, still strove.

28

Till, spent with toil, dreeing death for others,
　　And some whose hands should have wrought for *him*
(If children live not for sires and mothers,)
　　　　His mind grew dim.

And he fell far through that pit abysmal
　　The gulf and grave of Maginn and Burns,
And pawned his soul for the devil's dismal
　　　　Stock of returns.

But yet redeemed it in days of darkness,
　　And shapes and signs of the final wrath,
When death, in hideous and ghastly starkness,
　　　　Stood on his path.

And tell how now, amid wreck and sorrow,
　　And want, and sickness, and houseless nights,
He bides in calmness the silent morrow,
　　　　That no ray lights.

And lives he still, then ? Yes ! Old and hoary
　　At thirty-nine, from despair and woe,
He lives enduring what future story
　　　　Will never know.

Him grant a grave to, ye pitying noble,
　　Deep in your bosoms ! There let him dwell !
He, too, had tears for all souls in trouble,
　　　　Here and in hell.

·

The One Mystery

Ballad

'Tis idle ! we exhaust and squander
　　The glittering mine of thought in vain;
All-baffled reason cannot wonder
　　Beyond her chain.

The flood of life runs dark — dark clouds
    Make lampless night around its shore:
The dead, where are they ? In their shrouds —
    Man knows no more.

Evoke the ancient and the past,
    Will one illuming star arise ?
Or must the film, from first to last,
    O'erspread thine eyes ?
When life, love, glory, beauty, wither,
    Will wisdom's page, or science' chart,
Map out for thee the region whither
    Their shades depart ?

Supposest thou the wondrous powers,
    To high imagination given,
Pale types of what shall yet be ours,
    When earth is heaven ?
When this decaying shell is cold,
    Oh ! sayest thou the soul shall climb
That magic mount she trod of old,
    Ere childhood's time ?

And shall the sacred pulse that thrilled,
    Thrill once again to glory's name?
And shall the conquering love that filled
    All earth with flame,
Reborn, revived, renewed, immortal,
    Resume his reign in prouder might,
A sun beyond the ebon portal
    Of death and night ?

No more, no more — with aching brow
    And restless heart, and burning brain,
We ask the When, the Where, the How,
    And ask in vain.
And all philosophy, all faith,
    All earthly—all celestial lore,
Have but one voice, which only saith —
    Endure —adore !

A Broken-Hearted Lay

Weep for one blank, one desert epoch in
    The history of the heart; it is the time
When all which dazzled us no more can win;
    When all that beamed of starlike and sublime
Wanes, and we stand lone mourners o'er the burial
    Of perished pleasure, and a pall funereal,
Stretching afar across the hueless heaven,
    Curtains the kingly glory of the sun,
    And robes the melancholy earth in one
Wide gloom : when friends for whom we could have striven
With pain, and peril, and the sword, and given
Myriads of lives, had such been merged in ours,
    Requite us with falseheartedness and wrong;
When sorrows haunt our paths like evil powers,
    Sweeping and countless as the legion throng.

Then, when the upbroken dreams of boyhood's span,
    And when the inanity of all things human,
And when the dark ingratitude of man,
    And when the hollower perfidy of woman,
Come down like night upon the feelings, turning
    This rich, bright world, so redolent of bloom,
Into a lazar-house of tears and mourning —
    Into the semblance of a living tomb !
When, yielding to the might she cannot master,
    The soul forsakes her palace halls of youth,
    And (touched by the Ithuriel wand of truth,
Which oft in one brief hour works wonders vaster
Than those of Egypt's old magician host)
Sees at a single glance that all is lost !
And brooding in her cold and desolate lair
Over the phantom-wreck of things that were,
    And asking destiny if nought remain ?
    Is answered — bitterness and life-long pain,
Remembrance, and reflection, and despair,
    And torturing thoughts that will not be forbidden,
    And agonies that cannot all be hidden !

Lines on the Death of a Beloved Friend

I stood aloof : I dared not to behold
Thy relics covered over with the mould;
I shed no tear — I uttered not a groan,
But oh ! I felt heart-broken and alone !

How feel I now ? The bitterness of grief
Has passed, for all that is intense is brief —
A softer sadness overshades my mind,
But there thine image ever lies enshrined.

And if I mourn — for this is human, too —
I mourn no longer that thy days were few,
Nor that thou hast escaped the tears and woe,
And deaths on deaths the Living undergo.

Thou fadedst in the Spring-time of thine years —
Life's juggling joys and spirit-wasting fears
Thou knewest but in romance — and to thine eyes
Man shone a god — the earth a Paradise !

Thou diedst ere the icy breath of Scorn
Froze the warm feelings of thy girlhood's morn —
Ere thou couldst learn that Man is but a slave,
And this blank world a prison and a grave.

Thy spirit is at peace — Peace! blessèd word!
Forgotten by the million — or unheard;
But mine still struggles down this Vale of Death,
And courts the favour of a little breath !

Through every stage of Life's consuming fever
The soul too often is her own deceiver,
And revels — even in a world like this —
In golden visions of unbounded bliss.

But he who, looking on the naked chart
Of Life, feels nature sinking at his heart,
He who is drugged with sorrows, he for whom
Affliction carves a pathway to the tomb,

He will unite with me to bless that Power
Who gathers and transplants the fragile flower
Ere yet the spirit of the whirlwind storm
Comes forth in wrath to prostrate and deform.

And if it be that God Himself removes
From peril and contagion those He loves,
Weep such no more — but strew with freshest roses
The hallowed mound where Innocence reposes.

So may bright lilies and each odorous flower
Grow o'er thy grave and form a beauteous bower,
Exhaust their sweetness on the gales around,
And drop, for grief, their honey on the ground !

The world is round me now, but sad and single
I stand amid the throng with whom I mingle;
Not one of all of whom can be to me
The bosom treasure I have lost in thee.

Life and its Illusions

"Lean not on Earth — 'twill pierce thee to the heart —
A broken reed at best, but oft a spear,
On whose sharp point Peace bleeds, and Hope expires".
                                        — Young.

We are but shadows ! None of all those things,
Formless and vague, that flit upon the wings
Of wild Imagination round thy couch,
When Slumber seals thine eyes, is clothed with such
An unreality as Human Life,
Cherished and clung to as it is; the fear,
The thrilling hope, the agonising strife
Are not more unavailing there than here.
To him who reads what Nature would portray,
What speaks the night ? A comment on the day.
Day dies — Night lives — and, as in dumb derision,
Mocks the past phantom with her own vain vision !

33

Man shuts the Volume of the Past for aye —
A blind slave to the all-absorbing Present,
He courts debasement, and from day to day
His wheel of toil revolves, revolves incessant;
And well may earth-directed zeal be blighted!
And well may Time laugh selfish hopes to scorn !
He lives in vain whose reckless years have slighted
The humbling truth which Penitence and grey
Hairs teach the Wise, that such cold hopes are born
Only to dupe and to be thus requited !
How many such there be ! — in whom the thorn
Which Disappointment plants festers in vain,
Save as the instrument of sleepless pain —
Who bear about with them the burning feeling
And fire of that intolerable word
Which, inly searching, pierceth, like a sword,
The breast whose wounds thenceforward know no healing!

Behold the overteeming globe ! Its millions
Bear mournful witness. Cycles, centuries roll,
That Man may madly forfeit Heaven's pavilions,
To hug his darling trammels : — Yet the soul,
The startled soul, upbounding from the mire
Of earthliness, and all alive with fears,
Unsmothered by the lethargy of years
Whose dates are blanks, at moments *will* inquire,
"And whither tends this wasting struggle ? Hath
The living universe no loftier path
Than that we toil on ever ? Must the eye
Of Hope but light a desert ? Shall the high
Spirit of Enterprise be chilled and bowed,
And grovel in darkness, reft of all its proud
Prerogatives? Alas! and must Man barter
The Eternal for the Perishing — but to be
The world's applauded and degraded martyr,
Unsouled, enthralled, and never to be free ?"
Ancient of Days ! First Cause ! Adored ! Unknown !
Who wert, and are art, and art to come ! The heart
Yearns, in its lucid moods, to Thee alone !

Thy name is Love; thy word is Truth; thou art
The Fount of Happiness — the source of Glory —
Eternity is in thy hands, and Power.
Oh, from that sphere unrecognised by our
Slow souls, look down upon a world which, hoary
In Evil and in Error though it be,
Retains even yet some trace of that primeval
Beauty that bloomed upon its brow ere Evil
And Error wiled it from Thy Love and Thee !
Look down, and if, while human brows are brightening
In godless triumph, angel eyes be weeping,
Publish Thy will in syllables of lightning
And sentences of thunder to the Sleeping !
Look down, and renovate the waning name
Of Goodness, and relume the waning light
Of Truth and Purity ! — that all may aim
At one imperishable crown — the bright
Guerdon which they who by untired and holy
Exertion overcome the world, inherit —
The Self-denying, the Peaceable, the Lowly,
The truly Merciful, the Poor in Spirit!

So shall the end of thine all-perfect plan
At length be realised in erring Man.

Life is the Desert and the Solitude[1]

It is the joyous time of June,
    And fresh from Nature's liberal hand
Is richly lavished every boon
    The laughing earth and skies demand;
How shines the variegated land —
    How swell the many sparkling streams !
All is as gorgeous and as grand
    As the creations wherewith teems
    The poet's haunted brain amid his noonday dreams.

---

1. Mangan afterwards attached the same title to one of his
translations from Ludwig Tieck (q.v.)

Falls now the golden veil of even;
    The vault on high, the intense profound,
Breaks into all the hues of heaven;
    I see far off the mountains crowned
With glory — I behold around
    Enough of summer's power to mould
The breast not altogether bound
      By grief to thoughts whose uncontrolled
      Fervour leaves feeling dumb and human utterance
        cold.

Yet I am far — oh ! far from feeling
    The life, the thrilling glow, the power
Which have their dwelling in the healing
    And holy influence of the hour.
Affliction is my doom and dower;
    And cares, in many a darkening throng,
Like night-clouds round a ruin, lour
      Over a soul which (never strong
      To stem the side of ill) will not resist them long.

And all tnat glances on my vision,
    Inanimate or breathing, rife
With voiceless beauty, half Elysian,
    Of youthful and exuberant life,
Serves but to nurse the sleepless strife
    Within — arousing the keen thought,
Quick-born, which stabbeth like a knife,
      And wakes anticipations fraught
      With heaviest hues of gloom from memory's
        pictures wrought.

What slakeless strife is still consuming
    This martyred heart from day to day ?
Lies not the bower where love was blooming
    Time-trampled into long decay ?
Alas ! when hope's illusive ray
    Plays round our paths, the bright deceiver
Allures us only to betray,
      Leaving us thenceforth wanderers ever,
      Forlorn along the shores of life's all-troubled river.

Had I but dreamed in younger years
 That time should paralyse and bow
Me thus—thus fill mine eyes with tears—
 Thus chill my soul and cloud my brow!
No! I had not been breathing now—
 This heart had long ago been broken;
I had not lived to witness how
 Deeply and bitterly each token
 Of bygone joy will yield what misery hath bespoken.

Alas! for those who stand alone—
 The shrouded few who feel and know
What none beside have felt and known
 To all of such a mould below
Is born an undeparting woe,
 Beheld by none and shared with none—
A cankering worm whose work is slow,
 But gnaws the heart-strings one by one,
 And drains the bosom's blood till the last drop
  be gone.

Twenty Golden Years Ago

O, the rain, the weary, dreary rain,
 How it plashes on the window-sill!
Night, I guess too, must be on the wane,
 Strass and Gass[1] around are grown so still.
Here I sit, with coffee in my cup—
 Ah! 'twas rarely I beheld it flow
In the taverns where I loved to sup
 Twenty golden years ago!

Twenty years ago, alas! — but stay,
 On my life, 'tis half-past twelve o'clock!
After all, the hours *do* slip away—
 Come, here goes to burn another block!
For the night, or morn, is wet and cold,
 And my fire is dwindling rather low: —
I had fire enough, when young and bold,
 Twenty golden years ago!

1. Street and Lane.

Dear! I don't feel well at all, somehow:
    Few in Weimar dream how bad I am;
Floods of tears grow common with me now,
        High-Dutch floods, that Reason cannot dam.
Doctors think I'll neither live nor thrive
        If I mope at home so—I don't know—
Am I living *now*? I *was* alive
        Twenty golden years ago.

Wifeless, friendless, flagonless, alone,
        Not quite bookless, though, unless I chuse,
Left with nought to do, except to groan,
        Not a soul to woo, except the Muse—
O! this, this is hard for *me* to bear,
        Me, who whilome lived so much *en haut,*
Me, who broke all hearts like chinawear
        Twenty golden years ago!

P'rhaps 'tis better:—Time's defacing waves
        Long have quenched the radiance of my brow—
They who curse me nightly from their graves
        Scarce could love me were they living now;
But my loneliness hath darker ills—
        Such dun-duns as Conscience, Thought and Co.,
Awful Gorgons! worse than tailors' bills
        Twenty golden years ago!

Did I paint a fifth of what I feel,
        O, how plaintive you would ween I was!
But I won't, albeit I have a deal
        More to wail about than Kerner has!
Kerner's tears are wept for withered flowers,
        Mine for withered hopes; my Scroll of Woe
Dates, alas! from Youth's deserted bowers,
        Twenty golden years ago!

Yet may Deutschland's bardlings flourish long!
    Me, I tweak no beak among them;—hawks
Must not pounce on hawks; besides, in song
    I could once beat all of them by chalks.
Though you find me, as I near my goal,
    Sentimentalising like Rousseau,
O! I had a grand Byronian soul
    Twenty golden years ago!

Tick-tick, tick-tick!—Not a sound save Time's,
    And the windgust, as it drives the rain—
Tortured torturer of reluctant rhymes,
    Go to bed, and rest thine aching brain!
Sleep!—no more the dupe of hopes or schemes;
    Soon thou sleepest where the thistles blow—
Curious anticlimax to thy dreams
    Twenty golden years ago!

Siberia

In Siberia's wastes
    The Ice-wind's breath
Woundeth like the toothèd steel;
Lost Siberia doth reveal
    Only blight and death.

Blight and death alone.
    No Summer shines.
Night is interblent with Day.
In Siberia's wastes alway
    The blood blackens, the heart pines.

In Siberia's wastes
    No tears are shed,
For they freeze within the brain.
Nought is felt but dullest pain,
    Pain acute, yet dead;

Pain as in a dream,
    When years go by
Funeral-paced, yet fugitive,
When man lives, and doth not live.
    Doth not live—nor die.

In Siberia's wastes
    Are sands and rocks
Nothing blooms of green or soft,
But the snow-peaks rise aloft
    And the gaunt ice-blocks.

And the exile there
    Is one with those;
They are part, and he is part,
For the sands are in his heart,
    And the killing snows.

Therefore, in those wastes
    None curse the Czar.
Each man's tongue is cloven by
The North Blast, that heweth nigh
    With sharp scymitar.

And such doom each drees,
    Till, hunger-gnawn,
And cold-slain, he at length sinks there,
Yet scarce more a corpse than ere
    His last breath was drawn.

Very Interesting Sonnets[1]

To Caroline

I

Have I not called thee angel-like and fair?
    What wouldst thou more? 'Twere perilous to gaze
    Long on those dark bright eyes whose flashing rays
Fill with a soft and fond, yet proud, despair

1. Mangan's own title.

40

The bosoms of the shrouded few, who share
    Their locked-up thoughts with none: thou hast their
      praise;
    But beauty hears not their adoring lays,
Which tremble when but whispered in the air.
Yet, think not, although stamped as one of those,
    Ah! think not thou this heart hath never burned
    With passion deeply felt and ill returned.
If, ice-cold now, its pulse no longer glows,
The memory of unuttered love and woes
    Lies there, alas! too faithfully inurned.

II

For once I dreamed that mutual love was more
    Than a bright phantom thought; and when mankind
Mocked mine illusion, then did I deplore
    Their ignorance, and deem them cold and blind.
And years rolled on, and still I did adore
    The unreal image loftily enshrined
    In the recesses of mine own sick mind.
Enough; the spell is broke—the dream is o'er,
The enchantment is dissolved—the world appears
    The thing it is—a theatre—a mart.
    Genius illumines, and the work of art
Renews the wonders of our childhood's years;
    Power awes—wealth shines—wit sparkles—but the heart,
The heart is lost, for love no more endears.

Counsel to the Worldly-Wise

Go A-Foot and go A-head!
    That's the way to prosper;
Whoso must be carriage-led
    Suffereth serious loss per
Day in health as well as wealth,
    By that laziness with which
      Walkers have from birth warred;

41

And ere long grim Death by stealth
   Mounts the tilbury, and the rich
    Loller tumbleth earthward!

Also keep your conscience pure—
   Neither lie nor borrow;
He who starves to-day, be sure
   Always carves to-morrow.
March in front; don't sulk behind;
   Dare to live, though sneering groups
    Dub you *rara avis*—
"Serve your country—love your kind,"
   And whene're your spirit droops,
    Think of Thomas Davis![1]

The Night is Falling

The night is falling in chill December,
   The frost is mantling the silent stream,
Dark mists are shrouding the mountain's brow;
My soul is weary: I now
     Remember
The days of roses but as a dream.

The icy hand of the old Benumber,
   The hand of Winter is on my brain,
I try to smile, while I inly grieve:
I dare not hope or believe
    That Summer
Will ever brighten the earth again.

So, gazing gravewards, albeit immortal!
   Man cannot pierce through the girdling Night
That sunders Time from Eternity,
Nor feel this death-vale to be
    The portal
To realms of glory and Living Light.

---

1. This is the only tribute paid by Mangan to one of the noblest of Irish
patriots and poets.

Rest Only in the Grave

I rode till I reached the House of Wealth—
'Twas filled with Riot and blighted health.

I rode till I reached the House of Love—
'Twas vocal with sighs beneath and above!

I rode till I reached the House of Sin—
There were shrieks and curses without and within.

I rode till I reached the House of Toil—
Its inmates had nothing to bake or boil.

I rode in search of the House of Content
But never could reach it, far as I went!

The House of Quiet, for strong and weak,
And Poor and rich, I have still to seek—

That House is narrow, and dark, and small—
But the only Peaceful House of all!

Khidder

(This poem is founded on the same idea as that of another poem by
Mangan, "The World's Changes." *Khidder* is supposed by Mangan to be
the prophet Elias, whom the Persians or Arabs, or both, believe to revisit
the earth from time to time for the purpose of ascertaining the condition
of mankind.)

Thus said or sung
Khidder, the ever-young: —
Journeying, I passed an ancient town—
Of lindens green its battlements bore a crown,
And at its turreted gates, on either hand,
Did fountains stand,

43

In marble white of rarest chiselling,
The which on high did fling
Water, that then like rain went twinkling down,
With a rainbow glancing in the spray
As it wreathed in the sunny ray.
I marked where, 'neath the frown
Of the dark rampart, smiled a garden fair;
And an old man was there,
That gathered fruit. "Good father," I began,
"Since when, I pray you, standeth here
This goodly city with its fountains clear?"
To which that agèd man
Made answer—"Ever stood
The city where it stands to-day,
And as it stands so shall it stand for aye,
Come evil days or good."

Him gathering fruit I left, and journeyed on;
But when a thousand years were come and gone,
Again I passed that way, and lo!
There was no city, there were no
Fountains of chiselling rare,
No garden fair,
Only
A lonely
Shepherd was piping there,
Whose little flock seemed less
In that wide pasture of the wilderness.
"Good friend," quoth I,
"How long hath the fair city passed away,
That stood with gates so high,
With fountains bright, and gardens gay,
Where now these sheep do stray?"
And he replied—"What withers makes but room
For what springs up in verdurous bloom—
Sheep have grazed ever here, and here will graze for
    aye."
Him piping there I left, and journeyed on;
But when a thousand years were come and gone,

Again I passed
That way, and see! there was a lake
That darkened in the blast,
And waves that brake
With a melancholy roar
Along that lonely shore.
And on a shingly point that ran
Far out into the lake, a fisherman
Was hauling in his net. To him I said:
"Good friend,
I fain would know
Since when it is that here these waters flow?"
Whereat he shook his head,
—And answer made, "Heaven lend
Thee better wit, good brother! Ever here
These waters flowed, and so
Will ever flow:
And aye in this dark rolling wave
Men fished, and still fish,
And ever will fish,
Until fish
No more in waters swim."

Him
Hauling his net I left, and journeyed on;
But when a thousand years were come and gone,
Again I passed that way, and lo! there stood,
Where waves had rolled, a green and flourishing wood—
Flourishing in youth it seemed, and yet was old—
And there it stood where deep blue waves had rolled.
A place of pleasant shade!
A wandering wind among the branches played,
And birds were now where fish had been;
And through the depth of green,
In many a gush the golden sunshine streamed;
And wild flowers gleamed
About the brown and mossy
Roots of the ancient trees,
And the cushioned sward so glossy
That compassed these.

Here, as I passed, there met
Me, on the border of that forest wide,
One with an axe, whom, when I spied,
Quoth I—"Good neighbour, let
Me ask, I pray you, how long hath this wood
Stood,
Spreading its covert, broad and green,
Here, where mine eyes have seen
A royal city stand, whose battlements
Were like the ancient rocks;
And then a place for shepherds' tents,
And pasturage of flocks;
And then,
Roughening beneath the blast,
A vast
Dark mere—a haunt of fishermen?"

There was a cold surprise
In the man's eyes
While thus I spoke, and, as I made an end,
This was his dry
Reply—
"Facetious friend,
This wood
Hath ever stood
Even where it stands to-day;
And as it stands, so shall it stand for aye.
And here men catch no fish—here tend
No sheep—to no town-markets wend;
But aye in these
Green shades men felled, and still fell,
And ever will fell
Trees."

Him with his axe I left, and journeyed on;
But when a thousand years were come and gone,
Again I passed
That way; and lo! a town—
And spires, and domes, and towers looked proudly down
Upon a vast
And sounding tide of life,

That flowed through many a street, and surged
In many a market-place, and urged
Its way in many a wheeling current, hither
And thither.
How rose the strife
Of sounds! the ceaseless beat
Of feet!
The noise of carts, of whips—the roll
Of chariots, coaches, cabs, gigs—(all
Who keep the last-named vehicle we call
Respectable)—horse-tramplings, and the toll
Of bells; the whirl, the clash, the hubbub-mingling
Of voices, deep and shrill; the clattering, jingling,
The indescribable, indefinable roar;
The grating, creaking, booming, clanking, thumping,
And bumping,
And stumping
Of folks with wooden legs; the gabbling,
And babbling,
And many more
Quite nameless helpings
To the general effect; dog-yelpings,
Laughter, and shout, and cry; all sounds of gladness,
Of sadness,
And madness,—
For there were people marrying,
And others carrying
The dead they would have died for to the grave—
(Sadly the church bell tolled
When the young men were burying the old—
More sadly spake that bodeful tongue
When the old were burying the young)—
Thus did the tumult rave
Through that fair city—nor were wanting there
Of dancing dogs or bear,
Or needy knife-
Grinder, or man with dismal wife,
That sang deplorably of "*purling groves*
And verdant streams, all where young Damon roves
With tender Phillida, the nymph he loves,

47

And softly breathe
The balmy moonbeam's wreathe,
And amorous turtle-doves"—
Or other doleful men, that blew
The melancholiest tunes—the which they only knew—
On flutes and other instruments of wind;
Or small dark imps, with hurdy-
Gurdy,
And marmoset, that grinned
For nuts, and might have been his brother,
They were so like each other;
Or man
That danced like the god Pan,
Twitching
A spasmy face
From side to side with a grace
Bewitching,
The while he whistled
In sorted pipes, all at his chin that bristled;
Or fiddler, fiddling much
For little profit, and a many such
Street musics most forlorn
In that too pitiless rout quite overborne.
Now, when as I beheld
The crowd, and heard the din of life once more
Swell, as it swelled
In that same place four thousand years before,
I asked of them that passed me in the throng
How long
The city thereabouts had stood,
And what was gone with pasture, lake, and wood;
But at such question most men did but stare,
And so pass on; and some did laugh and shake
Their heads, me deeming mad; but none would spare
The time, or take
The pains to answer me, for there
All were in haste—all busy—bent to make
The most of every minute,
And do, an if they might, an hour's work in it.

Yet as I gave not o'er, but pertinaciously
Plied with my question every passer-by,
A dozen voices did at length reply
Ungraciously—
"What ravest thou
Of pasture, lake, and wood? As it is now
So was it always here, and so will be for aye."
Them, hurrying there, I left, and journeyed on—
But when a thousand years are come and gone,
Again I'll pass that way.

The Time of the Barmecides

(*From the Arabic*)

My eyes are filmed, my beard is grey,
    I am bowed with the weight of years;
I would I were stretched in my bed of clay,
    With my long lost youth's compeers;
For back to the Past, though the thought brings woe,
    My memory ever glides—
To the old, old time, long, long ago,
    The time of the Barmecides.
To the old, old time, long, long ago,
    The time of the Barmecides.

Then Youth was mine, and a fierce wild will,
    And an iron arm in war,
And a fleet foot high upon Ishkar's hill,
    When the watch-lights glimmered afar,
And a barb as fiery as any I know,
    That khoord or Beddaween rides,
Ere my friends lay low—long, long ago,
    In the time of the Barmecides;
Ere my friends lay low—long, long ago,
    In the time of the Barmecides.

One golden goblet illumed my board,
      One silver dish was there;
At hand my tried Karamanian sword,
      Lay always bright and bare;
For those were the days when the angry blow
      Supplanted the word that chides—
When hearts could glow—long, long ago,
      In the time of the Barmecides;
When hearts could glow—long, long ago,
      In the time of the Barmecides.

Through city and desert my mates and I
      Were free to rove and roam,
Our diapered canopy the deep of the sky,
      Or the roof of the palace dome—
O! ours was that vivid life to and fro
      Which only sloth derides—
Men spent Life so, long, long ago,
      In the time of the Barmecides,
Men spent Life so, long, long ago,
      In the time of the Barmecides.

I see rich Bagdad once again,
      With its turrets or Moorish mould,
And the Khalif's twice five hundred men,
      Whose binishes flamed with gold;
I call up many a gorgeous show—
      Which the Pall of Oblivion hides—
All passed like snow, long, long ago,
      With the time of the Barmecides;
All passed like snow, long, long ago,
      With the time of the Barmecides!

But mine eye is dim, and my beard is grey,
      And I bend with the weight of years—
May I soon go down to the House of Clay
      Where slumber my Youth's compeers!
For with them and the Past, though the thought wakes
            woe,
      My memory ever abides;
And I mourn for the Times gone long ago,
      For the Times of the Barmecides!
I mourn for the Times gone long ago,
      For the Times of the Barmecides!

The Time of the Roses

(*From the Turkish of Meseehi*)
Ob. 1512

Morning is blushing; the gay nightingales
Warble their exquisite songs in the vales;
Spring, like a spirit, floats everywhere,
Shaking sweet spice-showers loose from her hair,
Murmurs half-musical sounds from the stream,
Breathes in the valley and shines in the beam.
    In, in at the portals that Youth uncloses,
    It hastes, it wastes, the Time of the Roses!

Meadows, and gardens, and sun-lighted glades,
Palaces, terraces, grottoes, and shades
Woo thee; a fairy-bird sings in thine ear,
Come and be happy! — an Eden is here!
Knowest thou whether for thee there be any
Years in the Future? Ah! think on how many
    A young heart under the mould reposes,
    Nor feels how wheels the Time of the Roses!

In the red light of the many-leaved rose,
Mahomet's wonderful mantle re-glows,[1]
Gaudier far, but as blooming and tender,
Tulips and martagons revel in splendour.
Drink from the Chalice of Joy, ye who may!
Youth is a flower of early decay,
    And Pleasure a monarch that Age deposes,
    When past, at last, the Time of the Roses!

See the young lilies, their scymitar-petals
Glancing like silver 'mid earthier metals:
Dews of the brightest in life-giving showers
Fall all the night on these luminous flowers,

---

1. When Mohammed, says tradition, covered his head with the hood of his mantle, the covering shone like bright crimson wool steeped in oil.

Each of them sparkles afar like a gem;
Wouldst thou be smiling and happy like them?
    O, follow all counsel that Pleasure proposes;
    It dies, it flies, the Time of the Roses!

Pity the roses! Each rose is a maiden,
Prankt, and with jewels of dew overladen:
Pity the maidens! The moon of their bloom
Rises, to set in the cells of the tomb.
Life has its Winter:—When Summer is gone,
Maidens, like roses, lie stricken and wan;
    Though bright as the Burning Bush of Moses,
    Soon fades, fair maids, the Time of your Roses!

Lustre and odours and blossoms and flowers,
All that is richest in gardens and bowers,
Teach us morality, speak of Mortality,
Whisper that Life is a swift Unreality!
Death is the end of that lustre, those odours;
Brilliance and Beauty are gloomy foreboders
    To him who knows what this world of woes is,
    And sees how flees the Time of the Roses!

Heed them not, hear them not! Morning is blushing,
Perfumes are wandering, fountains are gushing;
What though the rose, like a virgin forbidden,
Long under leafy pavilion lay hidden;
Now far around as the vision can stretch,
Wreaths for the pencils of angels to sketch,
    Festoon the tall hills the landscape discloses.
    O! sweet, though fleet, is the Time of the Roses!

Now the air—drunk from the breath of the flowers—
Faints like a bride whom her bliss overpowers;
Such and so rich is the fragrance that fills
Æther and cloud that its essence distils,
As through thin lily-leaves, earthward again,
Sprinkling with rose-water garden and plain,
    O! joyously after the Winter closes,
    Returns and burns[1] the Time of the Roses!

---

1.   And still when the merry date-season is *burning*—Lalla Rookh.

O! for some magical vase to imprison
All the sweet incense that yet has not risen!
And the swift pearls that, radiant and rare,
Glisten and drop through the hollows of Air!
Vain! they depart, both the Beaming and Fragrant!
So, too, Hope leaves us, and Love proves a vagrant,
　　Too soon their entrancing illusion closes,
　　　It cheats, it fleets, the Time of the Roses!

Tempest and Thunder, and War were abroad;
Riot and Turbulence triumphed unawed;
SOLIMAN rose, and the thunders were hushed,
Faction was prostrate, and Turbulence crushed;
Once again Peace in her gloriousness rallies;
Once again shine the glad skies on our valleys;
　　And sweetly anew the poet composes
　　　His lays in praise of the Time of the Roses!

[1]I, TOO, MESEEHI, ALREADY RENOWNED,
CENTURIES HENCE BY MY SONGS SHALL BE
　　CROWNED;
FAR AS THE STARS OF THE WIDE HEAVEN
　　SHINE,
MEN SHALL REJOICE IN THIS CAROL OF MINE.
LEILA! THOU ART AS A ROSE UNTO ME:
THINK ON THE NIGHTINGALE SINGING FOR
　　THEE;
　　FOR HE WHO ON LOVE LIKE THINE REPOSES,
　　LEAST HEEDS HOW SPEEDS THE TIME OF
　　　THE ROSES!

Night is Nearing

(*From the Persian*)

Allah Akbar![2]
All things vanish after brief careering;
Down one gulf Life's myriad barks are steering;
Headlong mortal! hast thou ears for hearing?
Pause! Be wise! The Night, thy Night, is nearing!
　　Night is nearing!

1. In the MS of Nasmi's Anthology this stanza is written in large and
　gorgeous characters—Mangan's Note.
2. Great is God.

Allah Akbar!
Towards the Darkness whence no ray is peering,
Towards the Void from which no voice comes cheering,
Move the countless Doomed—none volunteering—
While the Winds rise and the Night is nearing!
Night is nearing!

Allah Akbar!
See the palace-dome its pride uprearing
One fleet hour, then darkly disappearing!
So must all of Lofty or Endearing
Fade, fail, fall;—to all the Night is nearing!
Night is nearing!

Allah Akbar!
Then, since nought abides, but all is veering,
Flee a world which Sin is hourly searing,
Only so mayest front thy fate unfearing
When Life wanes, and Death, like Night, is nearing!
Night is nearing!

The Howling Song of Al-Mohara

(*From the Arabic*)

My heart is as a House of Groans
    From dusky eve to dawning grey;
        Allah, Allah hu!
The glazed flesh on my staring bones
    Grows black and blacker with decay;
        Allah, Allah hu!
    Yet am I none whom Death may slay;
I am spared to suffer and to warn;
        Allah, Allah hu!
My lashless eyes are parched to horn
    With weeping for my sin alway;
        Allah, Allah hu!
For blood, hot blood that no man sees,
    The blood of one I slew

54

Burns on my hands I cry therefóre,
All night long, on my knees,
                    Evermore,
          Allah, Allah hu!

Because I slew him over wine,
          Because I struck him down at night,
                    Allah, Allah hu!
Because he died and made no sign,
          His blood is always in my sight;
                    Allah, Allah hu!
Because I raised my arm to smite
While the foul cup was at his lips,
                    Allah, Allah hu!
Because *I* wrought *his* soul's eclipse
          He comes between me and the Light;
                    Allah, Allah hu!
His is the form my terror sees,
          The sinner that I slew;
My rending cry is still therefóre,
All night long, on my knees,
                    Evermore,
          Allah, Allah hu!

Under the all-just Heaven's expanse
          There is for me no resting-spot;
                    Allah, Allah hu!
I dread Man's vengeful countenance,
          The smiles of Woman win me not;
                    Allah, Allah hu!
I wander among graves where rot
The carcases of leprous men;
                    Allah, Allah hu!
I house me in the dragon's den
          Till evening darkens grove and grot;
                    Allah, Allah hu!
But bootless all!—Who penance drees
          Must dree it his life through;
My heartwrung cry is still therefóre,
All night long, on my knees,
                    Evermore,
          Allah, Allah hu!

The silks that swathe my hall deewán[1]
Are damascened with moons of gold;
Allah, Allah hu!
Musk-roses from my Gulistán[2]
Fill vases of Egyptian mould;
Allah, Allah hu!
The Koran's treasures lie unrolled
Near where my radiant night-lamp burns;
Allah, Allah hu!
Around me rows of silver urns
Perfume the air with odours old;
Allah, Allah hu!
But what avail these luxuries?
The blood of him I slew
Burns red on all—I cry therefóre,
All night long, on my knees,
Evermore,
Allah, Allah hu!

Can Sultans, can the Guilty Rich
Purchase with mines and thrones a draught,
Allah, Allah hu!
From that Nutulian[3] fount of which
The Conscience-tortured whilome quaffed?
Allah, Allah hu!
Vain dream! Power, Glory, Riches, Craft,
Prove magnets for the Sword of Wrath;
Allah, Allah hu!
Thornplant Man's last and lampless path,
And barb the Slaying Angel's shaft;
Allah, Allah hu!
O! the Bloodguilty ever sees
But sights that make him rue,
As I do now, and cry therefóre,
All night long, on my knees,
Evermore,
Allah, Allah hu!

1. Sofa. 2. Rose-garden. 3. Lethean.

The Soffees'[1] Ditty

I.

BISMILLAH! Thou are warned, O Soffee! that
mere outward austerities, however excellent
in themselves, will not make thee perfect.

Haircloth and vigils and fasts, and a vow against coffee,
Cleansers from sin though they be, will make no one a Soffee.
Much is essential besides the bare absence of sleekness,
Namely: Docility, Poverty, Courage, and Meekness,
Wisdom, and Silence, and Patience, and Prayer without ceasing:—
Such are the tone and the tune of the ditty that *we* sing.

II.

Bismillah! Beware lest thou live in the habitual
commission of any single sin; for, though the
sin itself may be slight, the constant repetition
of it renders it most grevious.

Woe unto those who but banish one vice for another!
Far from thy thoughts be such damning delusion, O brother
Pluck thy heart out, and abjure all it loves and possesses
Rather than cherish one sin in its guilty recesses.
Donning new raiment is nobler than patching and piecing:—
Such are the tone and the tune of the ditty that *we* sing.

III.

Bismillah! And, O Soffee! whensoever the glitter
of money meets thine eye, avert thy face!
It were better for thee to lodge a serpent in thy
bosom than a money-purse.

---

1. This sect, which dates from the tenth century, is one of the most austere
in the East. The members wear blue gowns.

Money (saith Seyd Ul-ud-Deen) eats the soul as a cancer,
Whoso loves money has more than the guilt of Ben-Manser.[1]
Wouldst thou, O Soffee! keep clear of the snare that entangles
Those whom at night on their couches the Evil One strangles,
Ask not and task not, abstain from extortion and fleecing—
Such are the tone and the tune of the ditty that *we* sing.

IV.

Bismillah! There is no strength or wisdom
but in God, the High, the Great! Thou, O
Soffee, art but a creature of clay; therefore,
indulge not in pride!

Cast away Pride as the bane of thy soul: the Disdainful
Swallow much mire in their day, and find everything painful.
Still in its cave shall the diamond beam on, because humble.
When the proud pillar, that stands as a giant, must crumble.
Stoop! and thy burden will keep, like the camel's, decreasing.
Such are the tone and the tune of the ditty that *we* sing.

V.

Bismillah! The devil, O Soffee! will doubtless
try to make thee very miserable. But be thou
consoled; for the seven hells are closer here-
after against those who descend into them here.

Art thou made wretched by memories, and fears, and chimeras?
Grieve not! for so were the Soffees and saints of past eras.
All must abandon Life's lodgings, but none who depart take
Any invalider passport to Hell than the heart-ache.
Satan enslaveth, and Pain is God's mode of releasing—
Such are the tone and the tune of the ditty that *we* sing.

---

1. Abou-Mogheedh-Huseyn-Ben-Manser-al-Halladj, a celebrated Arabian
magician and mystic of the ninth century. He suffered death under the
reign of the Khalif Moktader, for promulgating certain incomprehen-
sible metaphysico-religious doctrines concerning the nature of the soul.
—Mangan's Note.

VI.

Bismillah! It is good for thee to be much
  afflicted. As Suleymán-Ben-Daood hath said:
  The heart is made better by the sadness of
  the countenance.

Like the lone lamp that illumines a Sheikh's mausoleum,
Like a rich calcedon shrined in some gloomy museum,
Like the bright moon before Midnight is blended with Morrow,
Shines the pure pearl of the soul in the Chalice of Sorrow!
Mourners on earth shall be solaced with pleasures unceasing—
Such are the tone and the tune of the ditty that *we* sing.

VII.

Bismillah! As Man soweth so doth he reap;
  his thoughts and deeds come back to him in
  another world; and as these are good or ill
  so is he for ever happy or miserable. Ponder
  this well; and let each fleeting hour impress
  thee deeplier with the awful truth, that Time
  is the purchase-money of Eternity.

Life is an outlay for infinite blessings or curses—
Evil or Good—which Eternity's Bank reimburses.
Thou, then, O Soffee, look well to each moment expended!
So shall thy hands overflow, and thy guerdon be splendid,
When thy brow faces the wall,[1] and thy pangs are increasing—
These be the tone and the tune of the ditty that *we* sing.

---

1. Viz., that wall of the death-chamber which is in the direction of Mekka.
—Mangan's Note.

The World—A Ghazel[1]

(From the Ottoman)

To this Khan, and *from* this Khan,
    How many pilgrims came and went, too!
In this Khan—and *by* this Khan
    What arts were spent—what hearts were rent, too!
To this Khan, and *from* this Khan
    Which for penance man is sent to,
Many a van and caravan
    Crowded came—and shrouded went, too!
Christian man and Moslem man,
    Guebre, Heathen, Jew, and Gentoo,
To this Khan, and *from* this Khan
    Weeping came and weeping went, too!
A riddle this since time began
    Which many a sage his mind hath bent to.
All came and went, but never man
    Knew whence they came or where they went to.

Heaven First Of All Within Ourselves

(From the Ottoman)

I stood where the home of my boyhood had been,
    In the Bellflower Vale, by the Lake of Bir-ból;
And I pensively gazed on the wreck of a scene
    Which the dreams of the Past made so dear to my soul.

For its light had grown dim while I wandered afar,
    And its glories had vanished, like leaves on the gale,
And the frenzy of Man and the tempests of War
    Had laid prostrate the pride of my Bellflower Vale.

---

1. A ghazel is a short piece of Oriental poetry rarely consisting of more than thirty lines, and usually limited to ten. It is distinguished by the recurrence of one particular rhyme from beginning to end; in most instances the name of the poet is introduced into it.

                              —Mangan's Note.

I thought how long years of disaster and woe
  Scarce woke in my bosom one sigh for the Past,
How my hopes, like the home of my childhood, lay low,
  While the spirit within remained calm to the last.

Then I looked on the lake that lay deep in the dell
  As pellucidly fair as in summers gone by,
And amid the sad ruins of cottage and cell
  Still mirrored the beautiful face of the sky.

And I said, So may Ruin o'ertake all we love,
  And our minds like Bir-ból, abide bright evermore;
So the heart that in grief looks to Allah above,
  Still reflects the same heaven from its depths as before!

Jealousy

(From the Ottoman)

  "My darling, tiny, little girl,
    I'll give thee jewelled shoes and dresses,
  I'll give thee zones of silk and pearl:
    And tell me who has combed thy hair?
  I'll give thee kisses and caresses,
    And say, what youth has combed thy hair?"

  "O, by my word! O, by my truth!
    O, by the life of Ali Shah!
  Aminah knows no other youth.
    By all the times that thou hast kissed her,
  Her hair was combed by Zillalah,
    Her own beloved sister!"

  "My own, my whitest girl, I vow
    I'll bring thee sweetmeats sugared newly;
  And tell me, only tell me now,
    Who over-darked thine eyes with *kohl*?
  My white Aminah, tell me truly,
    Who over-darked thine eyes with *kohl*?"

"O, by my word! O, by my soul!
  O, by the soul of Ali Shah!
Myself o'er-darked mine eyes with *kohl*!
  'Twas given me by my own dear mother,
My whitest mother, Fatimah:
  I had it from none other."

"My playful girl, I'll give thee rings,
  And gold, and gems beyond comparing;
I'll give thee thousand costly things!
  And say, who bit those lips of thine?
Come, tell what Kuzzilbash so daring
  Hath bitten those red lips of thine?"

"O, by my love! O, by my life!
  'Twas by a bright red rose this morn
Give me by Zayde, my brother's wife,
  These guiltless lips of mine were bitten.
(For brightest rose hath sharpest thorn;
  This, as thou knowest, is written)."

"Thou crafty girl, I know thine art!
  Dread thou my wrath: I give thee warning.
But if thou wouldst regain my heart
  Speak, tell me who has torn thy shawl!
Say what young Galionjee this morning
  Tore thus in twain thy scarlet shawl?"

"O faithless, truthless, worthless jade!
  I have tracked thee, then, thro' all thy lying.
Away! No jewels, no brocade,
  No sweetmeats shalt thou have of me.
Away, false girl! thy tears and sighing
  Seem worse than even thy lies to be!"

Double Trouble

(From the Ottoman)

I am blinded by thy hair and by thy tears together—
The dark night and the rain come down on me together.

A New Moon

(From the Ottoman)

Darksome through the Night of Separation
Unto two fond hearts must ever prove,
Those twin sorcerers, Hope—Imagination—
Raise a moon up from the Well of Love.[1]

Breadth and Depth

(Schiller)

Gentry there be who don't figure in History;
Yet they are clever, too—deucedly!—
All that is puzzling, all tissues of mystery
They will unravel you lucidly.
Hear their oracular dicta but thrown out,
You'd fancy these Wise Men of Gotham must find the
Philosophers' Stone out!

Yet they quit Earth without signal and voicelessly;
All their existence was vanity.
He seldom speaks—*he* deports himself noiselessly
Who would enlighten Humanity:
Lone, unbeheld, he by slow, but incessant
Exertion, extracts for the Future the pith of the Past and
the Present.

Look at yon tree, spreading like a pavilion! See
How it shines, shadows and flourishes!
Not in its leaves, though all odour and brilliancy,
Seek we the sweet fruit that nourishes.
No! a dark prison encloses the kernel
Whence shoots with round bole and broad boughs the
green giant whose youth looks eternal!

---

1. Mokanna, the Veiled Prophet, and other Eastern imposters, claimed
to raise moons and stars, lights and voices from the depths of wells.
                                                      —Mangan's Note.

The Ride Round the Parapet

(Rückert)

She said, "I was not born to mope at home in loneliness,"—
    The Lady Eleanora von Alleyne.
She said, "I was not born to mope at home in loneliness,
When the heart is throbbing sorest there is balsam in the forest,
    There is balsam in the forest for its pain,"
      Said the Lady Eleanora,
      Said the Lady Eleanora von Alleyne.

She doffed her silks and pearls, and donned instead her
    hunting-gear,
    The Lady Eleanora von Alleyne.
She doffed her silks and pearls, and donned instead her
    hunting-gear,
And, till Summer-time was over, as a huntress and a rover,
    Did she couch upon the mountain and the plain,
      She, the Lady Eleanora,
      Noble Lady Eleanora von Alleyne.

Returning home again, she viewed with scorn the tournaments—
    The Lady Eleanora von Alleyne.
Returning home again, she viewed with scorn the tournaments;
She saw the morions cloven and the crowning chaplets woven,
    And the sight awakened only the disdain
      Of the Lady Eleanora,
      Of the Lady Eleanora von Alleyne.

"My feeling towards Man is one of utter scornfulness,"
    Said Lady Eleanora von Alleyne.
"My feeling towards Man is one of utter scornfulness,
And he that would o'ercome it, let him ride around the summit
    Of my battlemented Castle by the Maine,"
      Said the Lady Eleanora,
      Said the Lady Eleanora von Alleyne.

So came a knight anon to ride around the parapet,
    For Lady Eleanora von Alleyne.
So came a knight anon to ride around the parapet,
Man and horse were hurled together o'er the crags that beetled
    nether—
        Said the Lady, "There, I fancy, they'll remain!"
        Said the Lady Eleanora,
        Queenly Lady Eleanora von Alleyne!

Then came another knight to ride around the parapet,
    For Lady Eleanora von Alleyne.
Then came another knight to ride around the parapet,
Man and horse fell down, asunder, o'er the crags that beetled
    under—
        Said the Lady, "They'll not leap the leap again!"
        Said the Lady Eleanora,
        Lovely Lady Eleanora von Alleyne!

Came other knights anon to ride around the parapet,
    For Lady Eleanora von Alleyne.
Came other knights anon to ride around the parapet,
Till six-and-thirty corses of both mangled men and horses
        Had been sacrificed as victims at the fane
        Of the Lady Eleanora,
        Stately Lady Eleanora von Alleyne!

That woeful year went by, and Ritter none came afterwards
    To Lady Eleanora von Alleyne.
That woeful year was by, and Ritter none came afterwards;
The Castle's lonely basscourt looked a wild o'ergrown-with-
    grasscourt;
        'Twas abandoned by the Ritters and their train
        To the Lady Eleanora,
        Haughty Lady Eleanora von Alleyne!

She clomb the silent wall, she gazed around her sovran-like,
    The Lady Eleanora von Alleyne.
She clomb the silent wall, she gazed around her sovran-like;
"And wherefore have departed all the Brave, the Lionhearted,
        Who have left me here to play the Castellain?"
        Said the Lady Eleanora,
        Said the Lady Eleanora von Alleyne.

"And is it fled for aye, the palmy time of Chivalry?"
        Cried Lady Eleanora von Alleyne.
"And is it fled for aye, the palmy time of Chivalry?
Shame light upon the cravens! May their corses gorge
   the ravens,
        Since they tremble thus to wear a woman's chain!"
        Said the Lady Eleanora,
        Said the Lady Eleanora von Alleyne.

The story reached at Gratz the gallant Margrave Gondibert
        Of Lady Eleanora von Alleyne.
The story reached at Gratz the gallant Margrave Gondibert.
Quoth he, "I trow the woman must be more or less than human;
        She is worth a little peaceable campaign,
        Is the Lady Eleanora,
        Is the Lady Eleanora von Alleyne!"

He trained a horse to pace round narrow stones laid
   merlonwise,
        For Lady Eleanora von Alleyne.
He trained a horse to pace round narrow stones laid
   merlonwise—
"Good Grey! do thou thy duty, and this rocky-bosomed beauty
        Shall be taught that all the vauntings are in vain
        Of the Lady Eleanora,
        Of the Lady Eleanora von Alleyne!"

He left his castle-halls, he came to Lady Eleanor's,
        The Lady Eleanora von Alleyne.
He left his castle-halls, he came to Lady Eleanor's.
"O lady, best and fairest, here am I,—and, if thou carest,
        I will gallop round the parapet amain,
        Noble Lady Eleanora,
        Noble Lady Eleanora von Alleyne."

She saw him spring to horse, that gallant Margrave
   Gondibert,
        The Lady Eleanora von Alleyne.
She saw him spring to horse, that gallant Margrave
   Gondibert.

"O, bitter, bitter sorrow! I shall weep for this to-morrow!
    It were better that in battle he were slain,"
        Said the Lady Eleanora,
        Said the Lady Eleanora von Alleyne.

Then rode he round and round the battlemented parapet,
        For Lady Eleanora von Alleyne.
Then rode he round and round the battlemented parapet;
The Lady wept and trembled, and her paly face resembled,
        As she looked away, a lily wet with rain;
            Hapless Lady Eleanora!
            Hapless Lady Eleanora von Alleyne!

So rode he round and round the battlemented parapet,
        For Lady Eleanora von Alleyne!
So rode he round and round the battlemented parapet;
"Accurst be my ambition! He but rideth to perdition,
        He but rideth to perdition without rein!"
            Wept the Lady Eleanora,
            Wept the Lady Eleanora von Alleyne.

Yet rode he round and round the battlemented parapet,
        For Lady Eleanora von Alleyne.
Yet rode he round and round the battlemented parapet.
Meanwhile her terror shook her—yea, her breath well-nigh
    forsook her,
        Fire was burning in the bosom and the brain
            Of the Lady Eleanora,
            Of the Lady Eleanora von Alleyne!

Then rode he round and off the battlemented parapet
        To Lady Eleanora von Alleyne.
Then rode he round and off the battlemented parapet.
"Now blest be God for ever! This is marvellous! I
    never
        Cherished hope of laying eyes on thee again!"
            Cried the Lady Eleanora,
            Joyous Lady Eleanora von Alleyne!

"The Man of Men thou art, for thou hast truly conquered me,
        The Lady Eleanora von Alleyne!
The Man of Men thou art, for thou hast fairly conquered me.

I greet thee as my lover, and, ere many days be over,
          Thou shalt wed me and be Lord of my domain,"
                Said the Lady Eleanora,
                Said the Lady Eleanora von Alleyne.

Then bowed that graceful knight, the gallant Margrave
      Gondibert,
              To Lady Eleanora von Alleyne.
Then bowed that graceful knight, the gallant Margrave
      Gondibert,
And thus he answered coldly, "There be many who as
      boldly
              Will adventure an achievement they disdain,
                For the Lady Eleanora,
                For Lady Eleanora von Alleyne.

"Mayest bide until they come, O stately Lady Eleanor!
              O Lady Eleanora von Alleyne!
Mayest bide until they come, O stately Lady Eleanor!
And thou and they may marry, but, for me, I must not
      tarry;
              I have won a wife already out of Spain,
                Virgin Lady Eleanora,
                Virgin Lady Eleanora von Alleyne!"

Thereon he rode away, the gallant Margrave Gondibert.
              From Lady Eleanora von Alleyne.
Thereon he rode away, the gallant Margrave Gondibert.
And long in shame and anguish did that haughty Lady
      languish,
              Did she languish without pity for her pain
                She the Lady Eleanora,
                She the Lady Eleanora von Alleyne.

And year went after year, and still in barren maidenhood
              Lived Lady Eleanora von Alleyne.
And wrinkled Eld crept on, and still her lot was maidenhood,
And, woe! her end was tragic; she was changed, at length,
      by magic,
              To an ugly wooden image, they maintain;
                She, the Lady Eleanora,
                She, the Lady Eleanora von Alleyne!

And now before the gate, in sight of all, transmogrified,
   Stands Lady Eleanora von Alleyne.
Before her castle-gate, in sight of all, transmogrified,
And he that won't salute her must be fined in foaming
   pewter,
      If a boor—but if a burgher, in champagne,
         For the Lady Eleanora,
         Wooden Lady Eleanora von Alleyne!

And then no More

(*Rückert*)

I saw her once, one little while, and then no more:
'Twas Eden's light on Earth awhile, and then no more.
Amid the throng she passed along the meadow-floor:
Spring seemed to smile on Earth awhile, and then no more;
But whence she came, which way she went, what garb she
   wore
I noted not; I gazed awhile, and then no more!

I saw her once, one little while, and then no more:
'Twas Paradise on Earth awhile, and then no more.
Ah! what avail my vigils pale, my magic lore?
She shone before mine eyes awhile, and then no more.
The shallop of my peace is wrecked on Beauty's shore.
Near Hope's fair isle it rode awhile, and then no more!

I saw her once, one little while, and then no more:
Earth looked like Heaven a little while, and then no more.
Her presence thrilled and lighted to its inner core
My desert breast a little while, and then no more.
So may, perchance, a meteor glance at midnight o'er
Some ruined pile a little while, and then no more!

I saw her once, one little while, and then no more:
The earth was Peri-land awhile, and then no more.
Oh, might I see but once again, as once before,
Through chance or wile, that shape awhile, and then no
   more!
Death soon would heal my griefs! This heart, now sad
   and sore,
Would beat anew a little while, and then no more.

Gone in the Wind

(*Rückert*)

SOLOMON! where is thy throne? It is gone in the wind.
Babylon! where is thy might? It is gone in the wind.
Like the swift shadows of Noon, like the dreams of the Blind,
Vanish the glories and pomps of the earth in the wind.

Man! canst thou build upon aught in the pride of thy mind?
Wisdom will teach thee that nothing can tarry behind;
Though there be thousand bright actions embalmed and
   enshrined,
Myriads and millions of brighter are snow in the wind.

Solomon! where is thy throne? It is gone in the wind.
Babylon! where is thy might? It is gone in the wind.
All that the genius of Man hath achieved or designed
Waits but its hour to be dealt with as dust by the wind.

Say, what is Pleasure? A phantom, a mask undefined;
Science? An Almond, whereof we can pierce but the rind;
Honour and Affluence? Firmans that Fortune hath signed
Only to glitter and pass on the wings of the wind.

Solomon! where is thy throne? It is gone in the wind.
Babylon! where is thy might? It is gone in the wind.
Who is the Fortunate? He who in anguish hath pined!
He shall rejoice when his relics are dust in the wind!

Mortal! be careful with what thy best hopes are entwined;
Woe to the miners for Truth—where the Lampless have mined!
Woe to the seekers on earth for—what none ever find!
They and their trust shall be scattered like leaves on the wind.

Solomon! where is thy throne? It is gone in the wind.
Babylon! where is thy might? It is gone in the wind.
Happy in death are they only whose hearts have consigned
All Earth's affections and longings and cares to the wind.

Pity, thou, reader! the madness of poor Humankind,
Raving of Knowledge,—and Satan so busy to blind!
Raving of Glory,—like me,— for the garlands I bind
(Garlands of song) are but gathered, and—strewn in the wind!

Solomon! where is thy throne? It is gone in the wind.
Babylon! where is thy might? It is gone in the wind.
I, Abul-Namez, must rest; for my fire hath declined,
And I hear voices from Hades like bells on the wind.

Ichabod! Thy Glory Has Departed

(Uhland)

I ride through a dark, dark Land by night,
Where moon is none and no stars lend light,
   And rueful winds are blowing;
Yet oft have I trodden this way ere now,
With summer zephyrs a-fanning my brow,
   And the gold of the sunshine glowing.

I roam by a gloomy garden wall;
The death-stricken leaves around me fall;
   And the night-blast wails its dolours;
How oft with my love I have hitherward strayed
When the roses flowered, and all I surveyed
   Was radiant with Hope's own colours!

But the gold of the sunshine is shed and gone
And the once bright roses are dead and wan,
   And my love in her low grave moulders,
And I ride through a dark, dark land by night
With never a star to bless me with light,
   And the Mantle of Age on my shoulders.

A Song from the Coptic

(*Goethe*)

Quarrels have long been in vogue among sages;
   Still, though in many things wranglers and rancorous,
All the philosopher-scribes of all ages
   Join, *una voce*, on one point to anchor us.
Here is the gist of their mystified pages,
Here is the wisdom we purchase with gold—
Children of Light, leave the world to its mulishness,
Things to their natures, and fools to their foolishness;
Berries were bitter in forests of old.

Hoary old Merlin, that great necromancer,
Made me, a student, a similar answer,
When I besought him for light and for lore:
Toiler in vain! leave the world to its mulishness,
Things to their natures, and fools to their foolishness;
Granite was hard in the quarries of yore.

And on the ice-creasted heights of Armenia,
And in the valleys of broad Abyssinia,
Still spake the Oracle just as before:
Wouldst thou have peace, leave the world to its mulishness,
Things to their natures and fools to their foolishness;
Beetles were blind in the ages of yore.

Life is the Desert and the Solitude[1]

Whence this fever?
Whence this burning
Love and Longing?
Ah! forever,
Ever turning,
Ever thronging
Tow'rds the Distance,
Roams each fonder
Yearning yonder,
There, where wander
Golden stars in blest existence!

1. Mangan called a poem of his own by this name originally, eventually changing it to "Stanzas which ought not to have been written in Midsummer". — D. J. O'Donoghue's Note.

Thence what fragrant
Airs are blowing!
What rich vagrant
Music flowing!
Angel voices
Tones wherein the
Heart rejoices,
Call from thence from Earth to win thee!

How yearns and burns for evermore
My heart for thee, thou blessèd shore!
And shall I never see thy fairy
Bowers and palace-gardens near?
Will no enchanted skiff so airy,
Sail from thee to seek me here?
O! undeveloped Land,
Whereto I fain would flee,
What mighty hand shall break each band
That keeps my soul from thee?
In vain I pine and sigh
To trace thy dells and streams:
They gleam but by the spectral sky
That lights my shifting dreams.
Ah! what fair form, flitting through yon green glades,
Dazes mine eye? Spirit, oh! rive my chain!
Woe is my soul! Swiftly the vision fades,
And I start up—waking—to weep in vain!

Hence this fever;
Hence this burning
Love and Longing:
Hence forever,
Ever turning,
Ever thronging,
Tow'rds the Distance,
Roams each fonder
Yearning yonder,
There, where wander
Golden stars in blest existence!

The Saw-Mill[1]

(From the German)

My path lay towards the Mourne again,
But I stopped to rest by the hillside
That glanced adown o'er the sunken glen,
Where the Saw- and Water-mills hide,
Which now, as then,
The Saw- and Water-*mills* hide.

And there, as I lay reclined on the hill,
Like a man made by sudden *qualm* ill,
I heard the water in the Water-mill,
And I saw the saw in the Saw-mill!
As I thus lay still,
I saw the saw in the Saw-mill!

The saw, the breeze, and the humming bees,
Lulled me into a dreamy reverie,
Till the objects round me, hills, mills, trees,
Seemed grown alive all and every,
By slow degrees
Took life as it were, all and every!

Anon the sound of the waters grew
To a very Mourne-ful ditty,
And the song of the tree that the saw sawed through,
Disturbed my spirit with pity,
Began to subdue
My spirit with tenderest pity!

"O, wand'rer! the hour that brings thee back
Is of all meet hours the meetest.
Thou now, in sooth, art on the Track,
Art nigher to Home than thou weetest;
Thou hast thought Time slack,
But his flight has been of the fleetest!

---

1. This is generally thought to be an original piece, but Miss Guincy
tells me she has found a German original. — D. J. O'Donoghue's Note.

74

"For thee it is that I dree such pain
  As, when wounded, even a plank will;
My bosom is pierced, is rent in twain,
  That thine may ever bide tranquil,
    May ever remain
  Henceforward untroubled and tranquil.

"In a few days more, most Lonely One!
  Shall I, as a narrow ark, veil
Thine eyes from the glare of the world and sun
  'Mong the urns in yonder dark vale,
    In the cold and dun
  Recesses of yonder dark vale!
"For this grieve not! Thou knowest what thanks
  The Weary-souled and Meek owe
To Death!"—I awoke, and heard four planks
  Fall down with a saddening echo.
    I heard four planks
  Fall down with a hollow echo.

Childhood

(Salis)

And where is now the golden hour
  When Earth was as a fairy realm,
    When Fancy revelled
Within her own enchanted bower,
  Which Sorrow came to overwhelm,
    Which Reason levelled;
When Life was new and Hope was young,
  And sought and saw no other chart
    Than rose where'er
We turned—the crystal joy that sprung
  Up from the ever-bubbling heart?
    O! tell us where!

75

Man, like the leaf that swims the wave,
　　A wanderer down that rushing river
　　　　Whose torchless shore
Is spectre-peopled from the grave,
　　Can scarce, amid his whirl and fever
　　　　Of soul, explore
The treasures infant-bosoms cherish;
　　Yet feelings of celestial birth
　　　　To these are given,
Whose Iris hues, too deep to perish,
　　Surviving Life, outlasting Earth,
　　　　Shall glow in Heaven.

I see thy willow-darkened stream,
　　Thy sunny lake, thy sunless grove,
　　　　Before me glassed
In many a dimly-gorgeous dream,
　　And wake to love, to doubly love
　　　　The Magic Past!
Or Fiction lifts her dazzling wand,
　　And lo! her buried wonders rise
　　　　On Slumber's view,
Till all Arabia's genii-land
　　Shines out, the mimic Paradise
　　　　Thy pencil drew!

Youth burns: we run the blind career
　　Which they who run but run to rue;
　　　　Too fleetly flies
The witchery of that maddening year;
　　Yet will we not the track pursue
　　　　Where Wisdom lies,
For Manhood lours, and all the cares
　　And toils and ills of Manhood born
　　　　Consume the soul,
Till withered Age's whitened hairs,
　　The symbols of his Winter, warn
　　　　Us to the goal.

But thou, lost vision! Memory clings
    To all of bright and pure and fond
      By thee enrolled!
Mementos as of times and things
    Antique, remote, far, far beyond
      The Flood of old!
Yet oh! the spell itself how brief!
    How sadly brief! how swiftly broken!
      We witness how
The freshness of the lily's leaf
    Ere Autumn dies, and leaves no token—
      And where art thou?

The Grave

(*Mahlmann*)

Blest are the dormant
    In death: they repose
From bondage and torment,
    From passions and woes,
From the yoke of the world and the snares of the traitor—
The grave, the grave is the true liberator!

Griefs chase one another
    Around the earth's dome;
In the arms of the mother
    Alone is our home.
Woo pleasure, ye triflers! The thoughtful are wiser;
The grave, the grave is their one tranquilliser!

Is the good man unfriended
    On life's ocean path,
When storms have expended
    Their turbulent wrath?
Are his labours requited by slander and rancour?
The grave, the grave is his sure bower-anchor!

To gaze on the faces
Of lost ones anew,
To lock in embraces
The loved and the true,
Were a rapture to make even Paradise brighter.
The grave, the grave is the great re-uniter!

Crown the corpse, then, with laurels,
The conqueror's wreath,
Make joyous with carols
The chamber of death,
And welcome the victor with cymbal and psalter:
The grave, the grave is the only exalter!

My Three Tormentors[1]

(*Song of a Maniac*)

Three spirits there be who haunt me always,
Plaguing *my* spirit in sundry small ways.
One is apparelled in purple and red;
   He sits on a barrel—a chaplet of laurel
   Which ought to be mine, and *was* before he
   Robbed me of brains, and bread, and glory,
Wreathèd around his globular head,
And a royal and richly bubbling cup
   Of the blood that he drains from his victims' veins
In his hand, that shakes as he lifts it up!
      Oh, woe, woe,
      And sorrow,
         To me, to be
         His slave,
      Through every coming morrow,
      Till years lay me low,
   Low in an honourless grave!

1. These tormentors would appear from the verses to be Intemperance,
   Avarice, and (perhaps) Love; or Bacchus, Plutus, and Cupid.
                                                —Mangan's Note.

My second tormentor, a weazened old pigmy,
Delves in a mine, as though he would dig my
Grave, or his own—I'd hardly care which!
　His visage is wrinkled and dust-besprinkled,
　His clothes are in rags, yet he heaps together
　Bright gold by the bushel; one scarce knows whether
The hateful old hunks be poor or be rich!
His gold is ever before his view;
　He worships it, he, and alas! makes *me*
In spite of my conscience, worship it too!
　　　Oh, woe, woe,
　　　And sorrow,
　　　　To me, to be
　　　　His slave,
　　　Through every coming morrow,
　　　Till years lay me low,
　　Low in an honourless grave!

The third—oh! the third is a marvellous creature,
Infant-like, and of heavenly feature!
His voice is rich as the song of the spheres;
　But ah! what tragic unrest its magic
　Doth bring to the bosom who shall tell of?
　To me that voice has been as the knell of
Death and Despair through bitterest years!
And then, his bright but mischievous eyes!
　Their mildest glance is the wound of a lance,
'Neath which the heart's blank innocence dies!
　　　Oh, woe, woe,
　　　And sorrow,
　　　　To me, to be
　　　　A slave
　　　To these through every morrow,
　　　Till years lay me low,
　　Low in mine honourless grave!

The Lover's Farewell

(Kerner)

Slowly through the tomb-still streets I go—
    Morn is dark, save one swart streak of gold—
Sullen rolls the far-off river's flow,
    And the moon is very thin and cold.

Long and long before the house I stand
    Where sleeps she, the dear, dear one I love—
All undreaming that I leave my land,
    Mute and mourning, like the moon above!

Wishfully I stretch abroad mine arms
    Towards the well-remembered casement-cell—
Fare thee well! Farewell thy virgin charms!
    And thou stilly, stilly house, farewell!

And farewell the dear dusk little room,
    Redolent of roses as a dell,
And the lattice that relieved its gloom—
    And its pictured lilac walls, farewell!

Forth upon my path! I must not wait—
    Bitter blows the fretful morning wind:
Warden, wilt thou softly close the gate
    When thou knowest I leave my heart behind?

My Adieu to the Muse

(Kerner)
1830

Winter is nearing my dark threshold fast,
    Already in low knells and broken wailings,
Ever austerer, menaces the blast
    Which, soon a tempest, with its fierce assailings
Will swoop down on its unresistant prey.

The Iris-coloured firmament, whereto
Imagination turned, weeps day by day,
　　For some lost fragment of its gold and blue,
And the dun clouds are mustering thick that soon
　　Will overdark the little of the beams
Of that unfaithful and most wasted Moon
　　Of hope, that yet with pallid face (as gleams
A dying lamp amid grey ruins), wins
　　The cozened spirit o'er its flowerless path.
So be it! When the wanderer's night begins,
　　And the hoarse winds are heard afar in wrath,
He gazes on the curtained West with tears,
　　And lists disturbedly each sound, nor sees
Aught but dismay in the vague Night, nor hears
　　Aught but funereal voices on the breeze,
But when—his hour of gloom and slumber done—
　　He looks forth on the re-awakened globe,
　　Freshly apparelled in her virgin robe
Of morning light and crownèd with the sun,
His heart bounds like the light roe from its lair.
　　And shall it not be thus with me—the trance
　　Of death once conquered and o'erpast?—Perchance
I know not, but I cannot all despair.
I have grieved enough to bid Man's world farewell
　　Without one pang—and let not this be turned
　　To my disparagement what time my unurned
Ashes lie trodden in the churchyard dell.
For is not Grief the deepest, purest love?
　　Were not the tears that I have wept alone
Beside the midnight river, in the grove,
　　Under the yew, or o'er the burial-stone,
The outpourings of a heart that overflowed
　　With an affection worlds beyond control,
　　The pleasurable anguish of a soul
That, while it suffered, fondly loved and glowed?
　　It may be that my love was foolishness,
　　And yet it was not wholly objectless
In mine own fancy, which in soulless things,
　　Fountains and wildwood blossoms, rills and bowers,
　　Read words of mystic lore, and found in flowers,

And birds, and clouds, and winds, and gushing springs,
Histories from ancient spheres like the dim wanderers
  Whose path is in the great Inane of Blue,
  And which, though voiceless, utter to the few
Of Earth, whom Heaven and Poesy make ponderers
  Apocalyptic oracles and true.
My Fatherland! My Mother-Earth! I owe
  Ye much, and would not seem ungrateful now;
  And if the laurel decorate my brow,
Be that a set-off against so much woe
  As Man's applause hath power to mitigate;
If I have won, but may not wear it yet,
  The wreath is but unculled, and soon or late
Will constitute my vernal coronet,
  Fadeless—at least till some unlooked-for blight fall—
For, thanks to Knowledge, fair Desert, though sometimes
  Repulsed and baffled, wins its meed at last,
And the reveil-call which on Fame's deep drum Time's
  Hands beat for some lost hero of the Past,
  If mute at morn and noon, will sound ere nightfall,
Hard though the struggle oft be which is made,
  Not against Power throned in its proud pavilions,
Not against Wealth in trumpery sheen arrayed,
  But against those who speed as the Postillions
Of Mind before the world, and, in their grade
  Of teachers, can exalt or prostrate millions.
I have said I would not be an ingrate—No!
  'Twere unavailing now to examine whence
The tide of my calamities may flow—
  Enough that in my heart its residence
Is permanent and bitter: — let me not
Perhaps rebelliously arraign my lot.
If I have looked for nobleness and truth,
  In souls where Treachery's brood of Scorpions dwelt,
  And felt the awakening shock as few have felt,
And found, alas; no anodyne to soothe,
  I murmur not; to me was overdealt,
No doubt, the strong and wrong romance of Youth.
Less blame I for each lacerating error,
  For all the javelin memories that pierce
Me now, that world wherein I willed to mirror
  The visions of my boyhood, than the fierce

82

Impulses of a breast that scare would curb
    One ardent feeling, even when all was gone
    Which makes Life dear, and ever frowned upon
Such monitors as ventured to disturb
    Its baleful happiness. Of this no more.
My benison be on my native hills!
    And when the sun shall shine upon the tomb
Where I and the remembrance of mine ills
    Alike shall slumber, may his beams illume
    Scenes happy as they oft illumed before,
Scenes happier that these feet have ever trod!
May the green Earth glow in the smile of God!
May the unwearying stars as mildly twinkle
    As now—the rose and jessamine exhale
    Their frankincense—the moon be still as pale—
The pebbled rivulets as lightly tinkle—
    The singing-birds in Summer fill the vale
With lays whose diapasons never cloy!
    May Love still garland his young votaries' brows!
    May the fond husband and his faithful spouse
List to the pleasant nightingale with joy!
May radiant Hope for the soft souls that dream
    Of golden hours long, long continue brightening
An alas! traitorous Future with her beam,
    When in forgotten dust my bones lie whitening!
And, for myself, all I would care to claim
    Is kindness to my memory—and to those
    Whom I have tried, and trusted to the close,
Would I speak thus: Let Truth but give to Fame
My virtues with my failings; if this be,
Not all may weep but none will blush for me;
And—whatsoever chronicle of Good,
    Attempted or achieved, may stand to speak
    For what I was, when kindred souls shall seek
To unveil a life but darkly understood,—
Men will not, cannot, write it on my grave
    That I, like myriads, was a mindless clod,
    And trod with fettered will the course they trod,
Crouched to a world whose habitudes deprave
And sink the loftiest nature to a slave,
    Slunk from my standard and renounced my God.

They will not, cannot tell, when I am cold,
That I betrayed, even once, a plighted trust,
Wrote but a single vow in Summer dust,
Or, weakly blinded by the glitter, sold
The best affections of my heart for gold,
And died as fickle as the wind or wave;
No! they will not write this upon my grave.

The Mariner's Bride

(From the Spanish)

Look, Mother! the Mariner's rowing
His galley a-down the tide;
I'll go where the mariner's going,
And be the mariner's bride!

I saw him one day through the wicket,
I opened the gate and we met—
As a bird in the fowler's net
Was I caught in my own green thicket.
O mother, my tears are flowing,
I've lost my maidenly pride—
I'll go if the mariner's going,
And be the mariner's bride!

This Love the tyrant evinces,
Alas! an omnipotent might,
He darkens the mind like night,
He treads on the necks of Princes!
O Mother, my bosom is glowing,
I'll go whatever betide;
I'll go where the mariner's going,
And be the mariner's bride!

Yes! mother, the spoiler has reft me
Of reason and self-control;
Gone, gone is my wretched soul,
And only my body is left me!
The winds, O mother, are blowing,
The ocean is bright and wide;
I'll go where the mariner's going;
And be the mariner's bride.

To the Ingleeze Khafir Calling Himself
Djaun Bool Djenkinzun[1]

(Thus Writeth Meer Djafrit)[2]

I hate thee, Djaun Bool,
Worse than Marid[3] or Afrit,
Or Corpse-eating Ghoul!
I hate thee like sin,
For thy mop-head of hair,
Thy snub nose and bald chin,
And thy turkey-cock air;
Thou vile Ferinjee![4]
That thou thus shouldst disturb an
Old Moslem like me[5]
With my Khizzilbash turban,
Old fogy like me
With my Khizzilbash turban!

1. Mangan suggests that these lines were addressed to a sneering English
traveller in Persia in the seventeenth century. Does Meer Djafrit mean
mere chaff writ?—D. J. O'Donoghue's Note.
2. The Oriental poets up to the seventeenth century, as the Irish up to
the tenth, always introduced their own names into their poems.
—Mangan's Note
3. Evil Djins of a very powerful order.
4. European.
5. Literally Scarlet-head, the Persians wearing exclusively red turbans,
while the other Oriental nations commonly affect white.

I spit on thy clothing,
That garb for baboons,
I eye with deep loathing
Thy tight pantaloons!
I curse the cravat
Which encircles thy throat,
And thy cooking-pot hat,[1]
And thy swallowed-tail coat!
Go hide thy thick sconce
In some hovel suburban!
Or else don at once
The red Khizzilbash turban—
Thou dog,[2] don at once
The red Khizzilbash turban!

Thou vagabond varlet!
Thou swiller of sack!
If our heads be all scarlet,
Thy heart is all black!
Go on to revile
Iran's[3] nation and race
In thy fish-foggish style!
He who knows with what face
Thou canst curse and traduce
Thine own mufti Pope Urban,[4]
May scorn thine abuse
Of the Khizzilbash turban—
Scorn all thine abuse
Of the Khizzilbash turban!

---

1. Major Skinner informs us that during his travels in the East his hat
   procured for him the title of "The Father of the Cooking Pot."
   —Mangan's Note
2. Ei Gaour! (In the Irish A Gadhar!).
3. Iran is the ancient name of Persia.
4. From this line it is clear that these verses cannot be older than the
   earlier part of the seventeenth century, as Pope Urban VIII (the last
   of the name) deceased in 1644. — Mangan's Note

The Domiciliary Visit

(A Scene in the Faubourg St. Antoine, Paris)

DRAMATIS PERSONAE — An officer of the Gendarmerie and
a Citizen.

Off.   *De par le Roi.* You are Pierre Coulisse!

Cit.   I am.

Off.   I thought so. Scan date,
       Address, and signature of this!
                                    (Gives him a paper.)

Cit.   *(reads)* "Arrest — by Royal mandate . . ."
       Why, what's my crime? *J'ignore* — —

Off.   Poh! Poh!
       Of course, young man, you ignore it —
           Your name is in the Black Book, though,
       With two red marks before it!
           Whence came you by those four cane-swords?

Cit.   Cane-swords? Which?

Off.   Yonder sham-rods!

Cit.   They are mere tobacco-pipes.

Off.   No words! —
       (Writes — "Two poniards and two ramrods"!)

Cit.   Heavens! You don't mean —

Off.   A Frenchman means
       The thing he does. Your press-keys!
                                    (Opens a drawer.)
       What make you with those tools?

Cit.   Machines.

Off.   Ay, such machines as Fieschi's![1]
       Pray, what's that carbine-like affair
       Behind the window-shutter?

Cit.   A walking stick.(*Il en a l'air.*)

Off.   Speak up, sir! What d'ye mutter?

Cit.   A stick!

---

1. I need not remind the reader that Fieschi is regarded as the inventor
   of the most terrific 'infernal machines' of modern times.
                                    —Mangan's Note

Off.   Don't shout! A lie's no truth
Because 'tis bellowed louder.
A gun you mean. A stick, forsooth!
Why, one can smell the powder!
(Takes up a book.)
Ha! "Treatise on the Poles"!

Cit.   The South
And North Poles only.

Off.   Rebel!
How dare you ope your *gamin* mouth?
Your explanations treble
Your guilt. South Pole and North? To what
Owes Earth its *revolutions*
If not to these, you leveller-flat
Of thrones and institutions?
Give up that letter! Ha! what's here!   *(Reads.)*
    "Dear Claude, I could not borrow
    One hour to-day; but never fear,
    I'll do the job to-morrow."
So-ho! The job? Oh, yes! — we hit
The meaning of such letters.
You'll do *the King's* job — eh? That's it!
Come, Jean, put on his fetters!

A Fast Keeper

My friend, Tom Bentley, borrowed from me lately
    A score of yellow shiners. Subsequently
    I met the cove, and dunned him rather gently;
Immediately he stood extremely stately,
And swore, 'pon honour, that he wondered greatly.
    We parted coolly. Well! (exclaimed I ment'lly)
    I calculate this isn't acting straightly;
    You're what slangwhangers call a scamp, Tom Bentley.

In sooth, I thought his impudence prodigious,
    And so I told Jack Spratt a few days after;
    But Jack burst into such a fit of laughter.
"Fact is," said he, "poor Tom has turned religious."
I stared, and asked him what he meant—
"Why, don't you see," quoth Jack, *"he keeps the Lent."*

A Thought

Though Laughter seems, it never is, the antithesis to
    Tears;
The gayest births of Circumstance or Fancy
But minister in masquerade to Sovereign Grief, who rears
    Her temple by that moral necromancy
Which fuses down to one dark mass all passions of Life's
    years;
And, as from even adverse facts Vallancey[1]
Proved us mere Irish to be Orientals,
Nature makes Grinning Schools turn men out
    Sentimentals.

Where's My Money?

(Franz Gaudy)

Ay! where's my money? That's a puzzling query.
    It vanishes. Yet neither in my purse
Nor pocket are there any holes. 'Tis very
    Incomprehensible. I don't disburse
For superfluities. I wear plain clothes.
    I seldom buy jam tarts, preserves, or honey;
And no one overlooks what debts he owes
    More steadily than I. Where *is* my money?

I never tipple. Folks don't see me staggering,
    Sans cane and castor, in the public street.
I sport no ornaments—not even a *bague* (ring).
    I have a notion that my own two feet
Are much superior to a horse's four,
    So never call a jarvey. It is funny.
The longer I investigate, the more
    Astoundedly I ask, *Where* is my money?

---

1. Charles Vallancey, a learned antiquary, who promulgated some queer
ideas as to early Ireland and the origin of the Irish people.
                                 —D. J. O'Donoghue's Note

My money, mind you! Other people's dollars
   Cohere together nobly. Only mine
Cut one another. There's that pink of scholars
   Von Doppeldronk, he spends as much on wine
As I on—every thing. Yet *he* seems rich,
   He laughs, and waxes plumper than a bunny,
While I grow slim as a divining-switch,
   And search for gold as vainly. Where's my
      money?

I can't complain that editors don't pay me;
   I get for every sheet One Pound Sixteen;
And well I may! My articles are flamy
   Enough to blow up *any* Magazine.
What's queerest in the affair though is, that at
   The same time I miss nothing but the *one*. He
That watches me will find I don't lose hat,
   Gloves, fogle, stick, or cloak. 'Tis always money!

Were I a rake I'd say so. Where one roysters
   Beyond the rules, of course his cash must go.
'Tis true I regularly sup on oysters,
   Cheese, brandy, and all that. But even so?
What signifies a ducat of a night?
   "The barmaids," you may fancy. No. The sunny
Loadstar that draws *my* tin is not the light
   From *their* eyes anyhow. Where then's my money?

However, *àpropos* of eyes and maidens,
   I own I *do* make presents to the Sex—
Books, watches, trinkets, music, too (not Haydn's),
   Combs, shawls, veils, bonnets—things that might
      perplex
A man to count. But still I gain by what
   I lose in this way. 'Tis experience won—eh?
I think so. My acquaintances think *not*.
   No matter. I grow tedious. Where's my money?

The Metempsychosis

(*Castelli*)

I've studied sundry treatises by spectacled old sages
    Anent the capabilities and nature of the soul, and
Its vagabond propensities from even the earliest ages,
    As harped on by Spinosa, Plato, Leibnitz, Chubb and
        Toland;
But of all the systems I've yet met, or p'rhaps shall ever meet
    with,
Not one can hold a candle to (*videlicet,* compete with)
The theory of theories Pythagoras proposes,
And called by that profound old snudge (in Greek)
    Metempsychosis.

It seems to me a pos'tive truth, admitting of no modi-
    Fication, that the human soul, accustomed to a lodging
Inside a carnal tenement, must, when it quits one body,
    Instead of sailing to and fro, and profitlessly dodging
About from post to pillar without either pause or
    purpose,
Seek out a habitation in some other cozy *corpus,*
And when, by luck, it pops on one with which its habits
    match, box
Itself therein instanter, like a sentry in a watch-box.

This may be snapped at, sneered at, sneezed at. Deuce
    may care for cavils.
    Reason is reason. Credit me, I've met at least one
    myriad
Of instances to prop me up. I've seen (upon my travels)
    Foxes who had been lawyers at (no doubt) some former
    period.
Innumerable apes, who, though they'd lost their patronymics,
I recognised immediately as mountebanks and mimics,
And asses, calves, *etcet'ra,* whose rough bodies gave asylum
To certain souls, the property of learn'd professors
    whilome.

To go on with my catalogue: what will you bet I've
    seen a
  Goose, that was reckoned in her day a pretty-faced
    young woman?[1]
But more than that, I knew at once a bloody-lipped
    Hyena
    To've been a Russion Marshal, or an ancient Emperor
      (Roman)
All snakes and vipers, toads and retiles, crocodiles and
    crawlers
I set down as court sycophants or hypocritic bawlers,
And there I may've been right or wrong—but nothing
    can be truer
Than this, that in a scorpion I beheld a vile reviewer.

So far we've had no stumbling-block. But now a puzzling
    question
    Arises: all the afore-named souls were souls of stunted
      stature,
Contemptible or cubbish—but Pythag. has no suggestion
    Concerning whither transmigrate souls noble in their
      nature,
As Homer, Dante, Shakespeare, Schiller—these now, for
    example,
What temple can be found for such appropriately ample?
Where lodge they now? Not, certes, in our present
    ninnyhammers,
Who mumble rhymes that seem to've been concocted by their
    Gammers.

Well, then, you see, it comes to this—and after huge
    reflection
    Here's what I say: A soul that gains, by many trans-
      migrations,
The summit, apex, pinnacle, or acmé of perfection,
    There ends, concludes and terminates its earthly
      per'grinations.

---

1. The transmigration of the souls of princesses into the bodies of owls
   has always been a matter of course; upon what principle it is not
   easy to divine.   —Mangan's Note

Then, like an air-balloon, it mounts through high Olympus'
     portals,
And cuts its old connections with Mortality and mortals;
And evidence to back me here I don't know any stronger
Than that the truly Great and Good are found on Earth no
     longer.

The Devil and the Wind

(From the Rheinsagen)

A LEGEND

I.

Before the Jesuits' House at Bonn the Wind pipes high and shrill,
It pipes all day, it wails all night — 'tis never, never still:
It shrieketh like a woman who hath not—or hath—her will.

II.

And why thus pipes, and why thus wails it, wails it night and day?
The cause is told in many an old and wizard monkish lay.
For ancient is that holy House, now falling to decay.

III.

The Devil, sadly tired of Hell, went once a-pleasuring forth,
And with him went his chosen chum, the wild Wind of the North—
When thus he spake—I give ye his words for what ye deem them
     worth:

93

IV.

"Good friend and faithful crony mine!—you mark that high House
    yon—
That is the Jesuits' Cloister-house, the far-famed House of Bonn;
And well and dearly love I, Wind, its dwellers every one!

V.

"So, you, my trump, just tarry here before the gate a space,
Just wait while I step in a bit, and glance about the place;
I want to see the Father Prior ament a conscience-case."

VI.

"Ha!" laughed the Wind, "that *must* be a Case of real Distress,
    no doubt!
However, you yourself know best — so, in with you, old Trout!
I'm safe to wait and whistle here until you again come out."

VII.

So said, so done: the Wind began its whistling there and then,
And in the Arch-Deceiver stole, to tempt the holy men —
Filled with all wiles and subtleties was he that hour, ye ken!

VIII.

"Hail, pious friends!" quoth he — "I've got a conscience-case to
    moot.
Pray, can I see your Prior's face?" — "Ay! and much more to
    boot,"
A monk replied, "if he, in turn, may only see *thy foot.*

IX.

"Avaunt, foul fiend! I know thee well! I guess thy crafty plot!
Begone! — But no! — thou shalt not hence: I chain thee to this
    spot!
Here shalt thou, till this House be dust, dree thine avenging lot!"

X.

The monk then chained Old Clootie down, despite his yells and
    cries,
And from that day—the Bonnsmen say—in thraldom thus he lies,
Because, from dread of direr dole, he dares not try to rise.

XI.

Meanwhile the Wind still waits without, and pipes in woful strain—
It whistles now — it howls anon — it storms, but all in vain.
Three hundred years have rolled, but Satan comes not forth again!

XII.

And Time and Hell go on to swell the victories both have won,
And many a generation since of monks has come and gone,
But still before that Cloister wails the wonder-wind of Bonn!

Haroun Al-Rashid and the Dust

(*From the Ottoman*)

I am but dust, said Hassan, as he bowed
    His face to earth abashéd;
And in my Khalif's glance I flourish or I wither!
Since you are only dust, replied aloud
    The great Haroun Al-Rashid,
Be good enough to say what wind has blown you hither!

Shapes and Signs

I see black dragons mount the sky,
 I see earth yawn beneath my feet—
  I feel within the asp, the worm
That will not sleep and cannot die,
 Fair though may show the winding sheet!
  I hear all night as through a storm
  Hoarse voices calling, calling
   My name upon the wind—
  All omens monstrous and appalling
   Affright my guilty mind.

I exult alone in one wild hour—
 That hour in which the red cup drowns
  The memories it anon renews
In ghastlier guise, in fiercer power—
 Then Fancy brings me golden crowns,
  And visions of all brilliant hues
  Lap my lost soul in gladness,
   Until I wake again,
  And the dark lava-fires of madness
   Once more sweep through my brain.